D1074776

TWAYNE'S WORLD AUTHORS SERIES
A Survey of the World's Literature

FRANCE

Maxwell A. Smith, Guerry Professor of French, Emeritus
The University of Chattanooga
Former Visiting Professor in Modern
Languages, The Florida-State University

EDITOR

Charles-Ferdinand Ramuz

TWAS 512

CRAMUY

CHARLES-FERDINAND RAMUZ

By DAVID BEVAN

Acadia University

TWAYNE PUBLISHERS
A DIVISION OF G. K. HALL & Co., BOSTON

Bevan, David, 1943–
Charles-Ferdinand Ramuz.

(Twayne's world authors series ; TWAS 512 : France)
Bibliography: p. 133–36
Includes index.
1. Ramuz, Charles Ferdinand, 1878–1947—Criticism
and interpretation.
PQ2635.A35Z557 1979   848'.9'1209   78-24499
ISBN 0-8057-6353-8

Contents

About the Author

Professor David Bevan was born in Gloucester, England and received his first degree from the University of Leeds. Thereafter he completed Master's degrees both at the University of Cape Town, South Africa and the University of Grenoble, France, before gaining his doctoral degree at the University of South Africa.

He has taught in the French Departments of three South African Universities, at Cape Town, Natal and Port Elizabeth, as well as at University College, Dublin, Eire. He is currently Head of the French Department at Acadia University, Nova Scotia.

Professor Bevan's main research interest is the narrative of the twentieth century and he has published and lectured widely in this area. An earlier book entitled *The Art and Poetry of Ramuz,* collaboration in a work on *Malraux* at L'Herne, and articles in *Nottingham French Studies, Bulletin de Grenoble, Standpunte, Cahiers de l'AFSSA, Twentieth Century Literature, Literature/Film Quarterly* are a selection from this activity. He is currently completing a study of the evolution of Malraux's narrative technique.

Preface

There can be few writers of merit who have languished so long in such widespread shadow as the Swiss novelist Charles-Ferdinand Ramuz. Acknowledged generally within the country of his birth as the leading Swiss literary figure of the twentieth century, he is still undeservedly ignored by too many critics in metropolitan France, for several of whom, sadly, there is little that is worthwhile to be found in the French language beyond the walls of Paris. But, perhaps the strangest and most tragic enigma of all is the almost total disinterest manifested until recently towards Ramuz in Anglo-Saxon countries, where he has rarely enjoyed more than a brief footnote in a chapter of Giono's regionalism.

And yet, far from being a regionalist author, Ramuz should rather be considered as amongst the most universal of writers, with an intuitive central belief in a fundamental creative capacity in all men, which transcends all frontiers, temporal or spatial. However, despite their continuing force in our invertebrate world, it is not primarily for his ideas that some concerned researchers are now beginning to reexamine a writer whose entire life was devoted to the search for an exact coherence between a vision of the world and the chosen means of expression. Indeed, it is not unreasonable to suggest that Ramuz's remarkable narrative technique situates him firmly in the forefront of that generation of experimentalist writers who so dominated much of the European literature of the nineteen-twenties, alongside more familiar names like Gide, Woolf, and Joyce. Although others have been more visible in their sophistications, Ramuz demands our attention for the discreet but total integration of subject matter and style which his best novels demonstrate. Never has it been more destructive to separate the aesthetic from the moral, as I shall shortly be forced to attempt in a critical vivisection.

It may be projected that it is almost entirely a lack of awareness of the importance of this unity which has prevented Ramuz from gaining the recognition he merits, especially in Anglophone countries. For the translations that exist at present are lamentable, mere factual approximations, an unacceptable impoverishment of the original work. When the immense complexities of the translation of an exceptionally polished style are avoided or neglected, then clearly the author in question will not be seen to any advantage at all. And even in the French, the unwary reader may well fail to give due weight to subtle forms and rhythms essential to the totality of the work.

It is this same inadequacy of available translated material which poses certain procedural problems to anyone attempting a book on the Swiss author entirely in English. Firstly, each extracted passage has to be translated anew; and, secondly, the original French must frequently appear as well, however cumbersome, in order to provide for those very many cases where either the translation is rather less than perfect, or else where the English language just does not possess stylistic resources identical to those of the source language. Without such referential inclusions the terms of the critical discourse may well be less than clear. Finally, the general lack of intimate acquaintance with Ramuz's writings requires a wealth of illustrative textual material which would not have been as vital to a study of an author where one was entitled to presuppose more.

With regard to the actual structuring of this present study I have for the most part traced Ramuz's itinerary, both material and artistic, chronologically and factually, but have deemed it worthwhile to focus rather more carefully on the mature novels in order to try to delineate—and unashamedly to admire—the qualities of the Vaudois novelist's art at its best.

It would be ungrateful of me to omit to mention in conclusion that the impetus for this analysis came from a stay of several years in South Africa: strangely enough, despite its small population, the English-speaking country where possibly Ramuz is best known, for the early links established by generations of Swiss missionaries survive and prosper today. Indeed, it was a Swiss scholar, Professor Pierre Haffter of the University of South Africa, who first guided my readings of Ramuz and without whose incisive advice and encouragement none of my work on that author would have been completed. There is a considerable intellectual debt, impossible to delimit with names, to many other outstanding academics of that much-criticised country, academics whose interest, stimulus, and help, often within the circle of the admirable Association for French Studies in Southern Africa, have always been in evidence.

Preface

I trust that the pages which follow will do justice not only to them and to the vision of the Twayne editors in inviting this book, but primarily to a writer who has yet to be admitted to the eminent position in twentieth-century European literature which he deserves to occupy.

Acknowledgments

The author would like to acknowledge his gratitude for having been accorded permission to quote from the following works of Ramuz: to Union Générale d'Editions in respect of *L'Amour du monde*, to Editions Gallimard for *Vie de Samuel Belet*, to Editions Grasset for *Jean-Luc persécuté, Joie dans le ciel, La Grande Peur dans la montagne, Farinet, Derborence, Le Garçon savoyard* and *Besoin de grandeur*. On all other occasions the rights to her father's works belong to Marianne Olivieri-Ramuz, and it is through her kindness that extracts from these have been able to be included.

Chronology

1878 September 24, Charles-Ferdinand Ramuz born at Lausanne. His parents are town-dwellers, but grandparents are from the country.

1894 Ramuz enters the local Gymnasium.

1896 Passes Baccalauréat examination.

1896– Six months' stay at Carlsruhe.
1897

1897– One term study in Law Faculty at the University of Lausanne, followed by the completion of an Arts degree (Licence).
1900

1898 "Conversation d'un soir d'été" published in the student journal *Zofingue—Noël*.

1900– First visit to Paris intending to prepare a thesis on Maurice de Guérin.
1901

1901 Teacher at College of Aubonne (Vaud) during the Michaelmas term but falls sick.

1902 Return to Paris. Teaches at the Ecole alsacienne in Rue Notre-Dame-des-champs.

1903 *Le Petit Village*, a collection of poems, is published at the author's expense in Geneva.

1903– Tutor to children of Count Prozor at Weimar.
1904

1904 Contributes prose-poems to the journal *Les Pénates d'Argile*. Other contributors were Adrien Bovy, Alexandre and Charles-Albert Cingria—the nucleus of that group which was later to produce *La Voile latine*.

1904– Domiciled in Paris, apart from spending summers in Switzerland. Lives successively at 5 Rue Sainte-Beuve (1904–5), 268 Boulevard Raspail (1905–6), 17 Rue Froidevaux (1906–8), 135 Boulevard de Montparnasse (1908–9), 12 Rue Liancourt (1909–10), 24 Rue Boissonade (1910–14). Begins in earnest a literary career.
1914

1905 Publication of *Aline*, his first novel.

1906 *La Grande Guerre du Sondrebond.*

1907 *Les Circonstances de la vie,* a novel that almost won for Ramuz the Prix Goncourt. First stay at Lens in the Valaisan mountains, frequently visiting the painter, Albert Muret.

1908 *Le Village dans la montagne.*

1909 *Jean-Luc persécuté.*

1910 *Nouvelles et morceaux.*

1911 *Aimé Pache, peintre vaudois.*

1913 Marriage to Mademoiselle Cécile Cellier, painter. *Vie de Samuel Belet.* Autumn pilgrimage to Cézanne's former residence near Aix-en-Provence.

1914 Publication of *Raison d'être,* a manifesto for Swiss-French writing, which constituted the first number of the *Cahiers vaudois* founded by Paul Budry and Edmond Gilliard. These journals were to become a rallying-point for a whole generation of exceptional artists in French-speaking Switzerland—the painter René Auberjonois, the composer-conductor Ernest Ansermet and writers such as the Cingria brothers, René Morax and Fernand Chavannes. Departure from Paris and installation at Treytorrens, near Cully. *Adieu à beaucoup de personnages* announces a new direction for his novels. *L'Exemple de Cézanne* continues both the ethical and aesthetic considerations of the preceding work. After the August mobilization he becomes a commentator on current events for the newspapers.

1915 *La Guerre dans le Haut-pays.* First meeting with Igor Stravinsky, which will lead to a collaboration in *Renard, Noces* and especially *L'Histoire du soldat* in 1918. Between October and January he gives a series of ten lectures at the Lausanne Conservatory on *Les Grand Moments du XIXe siècle français.*

1916 Moves house to "L'Acacia", Cour, Lausanne.

1917 *Le Règne de l'Esprit Malin,* which had already appeared in embryonic, serialized form between June and July 1914 in the *Mercure de France. Le Grand Printemps* applauds the Russian revolution, as does his article "A propos de Russie" in *La Semaine littéraire* on March 17th. *La Guérison des maladies.*

1918 September 28, collaborates with Igor Stravinsky (music) and

René Auberjonois (décor) to produce the spectacle *L'Histoire du soldat.*

1919   *Les Signes parmi nous* published by the *Cahiers vaudois*, now a publishing-house in its own right. The disappearance of the Cahiers as a review encouraged Ramuz to contribute generously to the *Revue romande* which had been founded in 1917. He withdrew his support however in December 1919 because of the journal's increasingly Maurassian political orientation.

1920   *Chant de notre Rhône.* The Schiller Foundation purchases the manuscript of *Aimé Pache, peintre vaudois.*

1921   *Salutation paysanne*, a collection of short pieces.

1922   *Présence de la mort. La Séparation des races.* Ramuz is awarded a Schiller Foundation Prize of 2000 francs.

1923   *Le Passage du poète.* "Hommage au Major", a commemorative piece written for the occasion—celebrated at Cully on April 24—of the two hundredth anniversary of the death of Davel, the hero of Vaudois independence.

1924   In this year the recent friendship with Henry Poulaille is cemented when Grasset becomes his Paris publisher with a second editon of *La Guérison des maladies*, initiated by Poulaille. Ramuz is consecrated in *Les Nouvelles littéraires* by an interview with Frédéric Lefèvre in the famous series "Une heure avec . . ."

1925   *L'Amour du monde* appears in the prestigious collection "Le Roseau d'or", through the good offices of Jacques Maritain. In May death of Ramuz's mother, née Davel.

1926   Journey to Auvergne and the Rhone valley motivated by desire to know other rural groups, such as that centered around Henri Pourrat whom he visits. *La Grande Peur dans la montagne*, which had appeared the previous summer in serial form in *La Revue hebdomadaire.* Publication in *Cahiers de la Quinzaine* of an open debate on the controversial Ramuzian style—entitled "Pour ou contre C. F. Ramuz."

1927   *La Beauté sur la terre*, first volume published by the Swiss industrialist Henry-Louis Mermod, who will be a constant source of aid and encouragement thereafter.

1928   Swiss literary prize awarded to Ramuz (Grand Prix Romand).

1928– *Six Cahiers* includes "Souvenirs sur Igor Strawinsky" and the

1929   two important "Lettres à Bernard Grasset" in which Ramuz explains and justifies his style.

1929   Founding of the weekly journal *Aujourd'hui* by H.-L. Mermod, primarily as a mouthpiece for Ramuz.

1930   April 24, installation at "La Muette," Pully, where Ramuz will reside until his death.

1932   *Farinet ou la fausse monnaie. Adam et Eve*, first of Ramuz's works to be published in the *Nouvelle revue française* (November 1932–February 1933).

1933   *Une main. Taille de l'homme*, a considerable reflection on the place of man within a universe continually enlarged by the discoveries of science. An extract appears in July number of *Esprit*.

1934   *Derborence.*

1935   *Questions* continues the reflections on man commenced two years earlier in *Taille de l'homme*. At the request of Jean Paulhan he collaborates in *Mesures*.

1936   *Le Garçon savoyard*, which appears in pre-original form in *Vendredi* from March to May. In October receives the Grand Prix literary award from the Schiller Foundation.

1937   *Besoin de grandeur. Si le soleil ne revenait pas.* Honorary doctorate from the University of Lausanne.

1938   Lecture in the Salle Iéna at Paris in June on "Une province qui n'en est pas une," under the auspices of the International Association for French Writers. *Paris, notes d'un Vaudois.*

1939   *Découverte du monde*, reflections on his childhood.

1940   Begins the preparation of his *Oeuvres complètes*, an immense task which involves the re-working and revising of all his earlier works. May 20, first signs of a weakening in health. Birth of a grandson "Monsieur Paul", who will command much of the writer's attention in his last years.

1941   *Fragments de Journal (1895–1920). Choses écrites pendant la guerre (1939–1941).*

1942   *La Guerre aux papiers.*

1943   October, ill again. *Journal. René Auberjonois.* Gallimard republishes *Vie de Samuel Belet.*

1944   *Nouvelles.*

1945   Three months' hospitalization with a stone.

1946 *Les servants et autres nouvelles.* Health deteriorating
      rapidly.
1947 May 23, death of Ramuz.

CHAPTER 1

Clearing the Ground

I *The Countryside*

CURIOUSLY, in the light of much of what is to follow, it was in
Lausanne, where his father was a small-time businessman that
Charles-Ferdinand Ramuz was born on 24 September 1878. But
sizeable though it was, it must be admitted that Lausanne at the end
of the nineteenth century was still very definitely a predominantly
rural town, especially on those colorful market days which were to
linger so long in the author's memory. Moreover, it does not require
much biographical investigation to ascertain that Ramuz's real roots
were fixed solidly in the soil of the Vaudois countryside: his paternal
grandparents came from the village of Sullens near Cossonay, and
his mother's family were longtime "viticulteurs":

It is clear that I am not the son of countryfolk. I was born in the town, I was
brought up in the town; I only knew the countryside at first during the
holidays, and they were short. I am nonetheless the grandson of peasant
people on my father's side[. . .] the grandson and great-grandson of vine-
yard-workers on my mother's.[1]

So the withdrawal of his parents to the country, which coincided
with his passing the Baccalauréat at the age of seventeen, came as no
great shock or disturbance. The young Ramuz merely became even
more entranced by the antiquity and simplicity of the rural world he
now frequented. There is no doubt that the impact of this bucolic
reality was far more decisive a factor ultimately than any other single
experience:

Above all, for the first time, I encountered difficulty, for Nature is not made
only to be looked at. I saw that there is another way of experiencing Her,
and more deeply than through the eyes, it is with the body; I saw that the

17

earth produces nothing before one has fought it, without first having conquered it.[2]

This is perhaps his true "découverte du monde," the moment of
radical and vigorously physical awareness which was to condition
Ramuz's future itinerary.

Extracted from what he considers to be a framework of monotony,
his most vivid childhood memories were put down on paper with
transparent affection in later years; and it is no surprise that many of
these spring from the most fundamental rural activities of those
years, those very activities which recur with such solidity and substance in so many of his stories. A memory of a mole-catcher invokes
a mysterious, almost mystical, figure, seen with excited horror and
admiration as he goes through the ritual of trap-setting; or
elsewhere it is the work of his father's cooper, or the brick-maker
whose unchanging function is as real for Ramuz as it has been for so
many children over so many centuries:

Ah, it is a very old task and which has scarcely changed since the world
began, nor have the materials used, for already the little people to be seen
on Egyptian sculptures were doing it. And there are bricks too from the
time of the Tower of Babel, in Genesis, where it is said: "Come, let us make
bricks and place them in the fire." The same materials, the same tools and
not even tools, or only the beginnings of tools, for the real tools are the
hands, and the hands of man, they haven't changed.[3]

The comparative boredom and repetition of schoolwork, the
erudition devoid of sensitivity of many of his fellows, contrast sharp-
ly in his memory with the joy and release of holidays—holidays
walking in the mountain pastures next to Les Diablerets, holidays at
the wine-harvest near Ivorne. This contact with the elementary is so
significant an experience in Ramuz's formative years that it is impossible to overstate it; for the first time he became aware of life and
living:

I went to the beings and things which exist beyond us and independently
of us; I seemed to see them for the first time. For one does not only see with
the eyes, nor with the intelligence alone, nor even only with the heart, but
with all your parts at the same time, that is to say with all one's body, at last
completely alive.[4]

Indeed the enrichment of this experience gave a new impetus to the more ordinary instruction of the Collège, as from this vision of the total authenticity of rural life there grew slowly but decisively that realization of historical permanence which was to become the very life-blood of his later writings:

it was the space I inhabited which made time, too, begin to live for me [. . .]. The Greek poets that we continued to have to translate at school thus became my contemporaries.[5]

II *The Bible*

Undoubtedly the single book which had the most far-reaching influence on the young Ramuz, as he himself was to acknowledge so frequently in later life, was the Bible. From his earliest days at the Collège this was his most constant nourishment; he received a minimum of two hours' reading a week from the Scriptures—often stories which moved him passionately, stories he felt he saw reenacted all around him in his own land. These were people, events, and activities he was never to forget. Certainly, the Swiss-French community in the late eighteen hundreds was of devout Calvinist belief and no boy growing up there during those years could have failed to absorb the austere Christian ethic which that supposed.

But far more than as a divinely-inspired source of a faith and of a morality, it was as a storybook, as an anthology of unforgettable and enduring characters that the Bible impregnated his child's mind:

Genesis was for me, well before the *Odyssey*, a book full of fascinating stories that was read to us on Sunday mornings, from eleven to mid-day, in the Church of St. Francis. [. . .] A commentary used to be given on the chapter or part of a chapter for that day. But I have no memory of the commentaries, it is only the characters whom I see, Abram who became Abraham, Saraï who became Sarah, Noah and then his son who walks backwards in order not to see his father's nakedness. They emerge from the depths of time and yet were also in mine, just like our own country people, cultivating the ground and the vine like them. There was a wonderful harmony between that childhood of the world and our own childhood. All those stories in the Bible, I have experienced them.[6]

III *At School, Army, and University*

Apart from avidly embracing nearly all available reading material, Ramuz was from the very beginning easily distracted from everything "academic," a dreamy introverted child. At Mademoiselle

Dommer's private school in Lausanne from the age of five, through
Monsieur Pasche's preparatory school, both at the Collège and later
the Gymnasium, his results ranged only from mediocre to average,
in every subject except French.

While he was still in his early teens, despite usually tacit parental
opposition, his vocation, his very *raison d'être*, was firmly established. Inevitably at this stage his models were drawn from the
sacrosanct area of those readings to which he was introduced by the
patient, friendly, but unimaginative teachers of the formal Swiss
system. Ramuz himself remembers wryly in his revealing recollec-
tion of this period, *Découverte du monde*, several of his imitative
concoctions—a desperately conventional octosyllabic poem called *A
une étoile*, and a series of heroic five-act plays in collaboration with
one Hans Isher, a childhood ally.

It was undoubtedly the experience with M. Abel Biaudet, his
French teacher, which did most to encourage the young Ramuz in
his already firm conviction. M. Biaudet had proposed as homework
a free composition; and when Charles-Ferdinand produced a work
on Rome entirely in Alexandrines, the teacher, having first satisfied
himself of its authenticity, felt compelled to give his pupil a mark of
one hundred per cent. For the would-be-writer it appeared as a
sanction, a sign from above.

By his mid-teens it is clear that the essential elements of Ramuz's
future development were already present: the passionate embracing
of the Vaudois countryside and an almost sacerdotal reverence for
literature, as yet still cluttered by the insistent trappings of a traditional bourgeois education. It seems probable that already he
sensed his own worth, even glimpsed, without fully rationalizing or
developing, his future path as he wondered, "What would Aes-
chylus have done, if he had been born in 1878 somewhere in my
country, the land of Vaud?"[7]

However, the moment of material decision was not yet come. In
1896, at the age of not quite eighteen, Ramuz was successful in
passing his Baccalauréat; and, as was very much the custom of the
time, he decided to spend a few months away, at Carlsruhe, before
continuing at a University. Upon his return his father, still very
much opposed to the notion of a literary son, persuaded him rather
to enrol in the Law Faculty at the University of Lausanne. But, after
only two terms of utter boredom, Ramuz contrived with the growing
support of an affectionate mother to transfer to the more suitable
environment of the Faculté des Lettres.

His studies at this point were interrupted by the statutory period of military service. However, a time which might have proved painfully constricting to his fiercely creative mind was enormously enriched by a liaison within the regiment with a young man of considerable charm and flair, Alexandre Cingria. It was a friendship that was to last many years and embrace many artistic enterprises; but perhaps its greatest fruit was born from these early days when the enlightened Cingria, having just returned from Italy, introduced Ramuz to painting and thus stimulated a passion which was to color his literature throughout his career.

Upon completion of his service Ramuz resumed his Arts degree and in 1900 was awarded, as his citation supplies, "la plus moderne des licences classiques." Yet, far from resolving anything, this event only served to highlight an already difficult relationship with his father over the choice of a career, aggravated still further by Ramuz's departure for Paris in October 1900 with the apparent intention of preparing a thesis on the poetry of Maurice de Guérin.

Ramuz's *Journal* leaves us in no doubt that this was one of the most unpleasant periods in Ramuz's life—upset by family division, wracked by self-doubt, and disturbed by continual movement. His brief stay in Paris was followed by a few months as a German teacher at Aubonne before a bout of illness, appendicitis and peritonitis, finally struck him down completely for six months. But, happily it was this very period of forced inactivity which allowed him time to reexamine his own itinerary, and as soon as he had recovered he entrained once more for Paris where, apart from acting temporarily in 1903–1904 as tutor to the children of Count Prozor of Russia, he was to reside for the next ten or eleven years.

IV *Paris*

The importance of this sojourn to the evolution of the young artist cannot be overstated, for it was above all in Paris that he became aware of himself. The call of metropolitan culture was the stimulus, but in the event the outcome of this journey was very different. For it was only in absence that he became truly aware of the quality and the significance of his own country. Faced with his obvious foreignness Ramuz was simultaneously confronted by his identity with the race and the soil of his homeland.

The days at this time were divided principally between visits to galleries of the Louvre, for painting had already become a part of

him, and hours and hours spent poring over sheets of paper as he
strove for the right words. But this was a time of immense frustra-
tion and despair for, too frequently, the words failed to come:

And I shall only recognize this past day by the trace of some poor lines
thrown hastily onto the paper. I move in space, I stir my body, I stretch my
mind, I speak, I think; and nothing remains but a total disgust with this
nothingness. I thirst for the impossible and hunger desperately for the
absolute; where is the spring of fresh water, where is the wheaten bread?[8]

Torn in his creativity between his learned bourgeois background
and his yearning for unaffected simplicity, his diary of these months
is littered with evidence of an agonizingly uncertain dichotomy:

I don't know myself. I am trying to emerge from this mysterious twilight
where I am in danger of losing myself [. . .]. This uncertainty is devastat-
ing.[9]

Again and again the specter which haunts Ramuz, and which he
will go vigorously reject before long, is that of "demi-instruction,"
that stultifying rather than educating process which "takes away
originality by imposing on all these rudimentary intelligences common ideas which are most often only conventions and which take
over."[10]

Already it was not so much the subject matter of his writing that
was causing him such poignant concern, but the expression. His
contact with nature, and now the city, had made him vividly aware
of a common essence in man:

The mold in which Nature has cast man has infinite variations: but only in
its detail and the apparent form remains the same. The passions remain
identical in all centuries and in all countries. Not only do the purely vegeta-
ble functions recur in similar form and minutely perfected through the
whole scale of animate beings, but even the superior functions only vary
qualitatively.[11]

It was the wonder and beauty of this authentic and fundamental
humanity that he was seeking to express in all its fullness and
simplicity, and merely to express it would be reward enough:

may the living things in me come living from my mouth; and may all that is
beauty find me each day more attentive to its praises. I shall resemble the

little shepherd who sings on the mountaintop as he guards his flocks; no one hears him, but he is happy: he sings only for himself.[12]

V   Le Petit Village

Although the first concrete indication of a step forward, a renunciation of the poetic tradition he had espoused in his early years, is dated in his diary 19 December 1901,

That irregular rhythm which usually cuts off any inspiration had today remarkably facilitated the task; it was indeed the one which corresponded to my internal rhythm, it was therefore necessary; consequently it is good, although hardly distinctive from prose [. . .]. What does it matter even if it is contrary to preconceived notions.[13]

Ramuz nevertheless arrived in Paris clutching a bundle of bucolic draft poems in perfect Alexandrines—they were already entitled *Le Petit Village*.

But their pomp and artifice, the discord between "fond" and "forme," was now apparent to him; and the *Journal* informs us that on 10 January 1903 he abandoned them irrevocably, at least "according to the plan I had sketched out."[14] He adds, delightfully, in *Découverte du monde*, "I had dressed my village falsely, dressed it in Sunday best; I had busied myself in Paris, in re-dressing it in everyday wear."[15] It was in particular the rigid versification and insistent regularity that jarred:

those beautiful and very even Alexandrines no longer seemed to correspond to its particular nature and life; I needed to find another form, slightly uneven in gait, for it seemed to me from a distance that my country limped; quite happily clumsy, and a little gauche and uneasy as is a peasant in a large town.[16]

Perhaps even more apposite are those lines which appear in his *Journal* at this time and which again abhor the disparity between the unyielding classical poetic mold and the ingenuously banal prose of his subject:

It must be the rhythm which carries, which must be interior; as soon as the sentence must be broken up in order to get it into a mold already prepared, it loses its authenticity. I overburden with useless ornaments prose which, by an artifice of typography, has the appearance of verse.[17]

Ramuz rewrote his ponderous Parnassian lines in blank verse, replaced rhyme with gentle assonance, and gave to the style a freshness, indeed a nudity, which not only admirably suited the subject, but also gave early testimony to a considerable and original talent.

After being amiably but firmly rejected by the Librairie Rouge in Geneva, his manuscript was accepted at his own expense by Charles Eggimann of the same town. Happily for Ramuz's always slender finances, although the publishing cost was three hundred and fifty francs—given by a now tolerant father—the edition realized five hundred francs, and produced a welcome, if unexpected, profit of one hundred and fifty francs!

Even more welcome were the generous eulogies of several well-respected critics, for it was in no small measure their early consecration which effectively began to establish Ramuz as a new literary figure in French-speaking Switzerland. Although the less discerning tended to lose sight of the primacy of freshness and charm in the conditioned warmth of their response to a certain realism—"a minute and accurate observation of rustic life" wrote Philippe Godet,[18] "poetry of humble truth" agreed Fernand Chavannes[19]—only one, the inexorably pedantic Jules Cougnard of La Patrie suisse, lamented the unconventionality of the chosen form ("our ears have become used to habitual rhythms that are not to be broken with impunity").[20] Certainly the general tone of the pundits was not far short of Gaspard Vallette's highly favorable review which was published in La Suisse very soon indeed after Ramuz's slim volume first appeared:

Here is a little book far removed from the ordinary banalities. Out of the absurd torrent of literary mediocrity which the approaching New Year rains down upon us, this exquisite book of poetry, natural, direct, spontaneous and sincere, emerges as a vigorous plant in full flower. There is nothing Parnassian about C.F. Ramuz's lines, they are rather a form of prose with a sure and artistic rhythm. But the vision they express is so frank, so fresh that by simplicity itself, the author attains great beauty. Never has the life of a Swiss village been communicated with such charming truth and candor.[21]

There is little more to say about a series of fugitive impressions and sketches taken from the daily round of Vaudois village life. In each case, whether the subject be an old lady, the local mole-

catcher, a burial, or whatever, it is the air of utterly rural naïveté
which strikes one most vividly. Indeed nowhere more so than in the
delightful portrait of Jean-Daniel who, like so many others here, was
to reappear in more developed form and setting in Ramuz's later
writings:

"Portrait of Jean-Daniel"

> He is short and squat, he only has during the week
> to be able to work comfortably
> his shirt and heavy grey trousers,
> but on Sunday he dresses in black.
>
> He has wide shoulders, a bony face
> which is the color of the sun,
> a yellow moustache which smells of wine
> and small eyes, pale and quick.
>
> His speech is slow and rhythmic
> like his movement and like his gait
> as he walks evenly, quietly,
> looking at the sky above him
> to see the weather it will be,
> the deserted fields where the seed is growing,
> the land he loves, because it gives him life.[22]

VI *The Collaboration of* Les Pénates d'Argil

The encouragement of the critics, however, was soon to plunge
the insecure Ramuz, paradoxically, into even greater mental anguish as he became painfully aware that the fear of returning to the
abyss is greater the higher one climbs. With this as a constant spur
he redoubled his efforts, in the wake of *Le Petit Village*, to forge a
style not merely acceptable but perfect.

> But I persist, so great and tempting is this task of circumscribing, of fixing,
> and of remaining oneself; I devote to it my thoughtfilled nights and the
> somber work of my days;—at random, knowing myself poorly, uncertain of
> my limitations and of my potential, [. . .] seeking however, but always in
> the same direction, having been rebuffed everywhere else, until my head
> strikes the wall and I fall stunned.[23]

Happily, at this very point in time, a close collaboration of a creative type with several of his growing number of expatriate friends in Paris came to occupy a large part of his days.

The first idea, in late 1903, of a literary collaboration principally between Ramuz, the Cingria brothers, Alexandre and Charles-Albert, and Adrien Bovy—whom Ramuz had met en route for Eggimann's to publish *Le Petit Village*—was that of Alexandre Cingria. The title to be given to the enterprise, *Les Pénates d'Argile*, was however chosen by Ramuz himself from a La Fontaine fable.

It is not surprising that Ramuz's own contributions appear somewhat similar to the pieces of the almost contemporary *Le Petit Village*, sixteen prose poems devoid of narrative, mere glimpses. Indeed he willingly admits in his diary at this time his refusal of the anecdotal and confesses,

a discontinuity of thought which makes me see the world by successive shocks, sparks and flashes, scattered fragments which follow each other without any link of continuity.[24]

But there was to be one important difference. Their lofty aim of regenerating Swiss-French letters had as its chief and regrettable effect to suggest to the collaborators the need to demonstrate their learning, culture, and intelligence. This they certainly achieved, witness the words of the Countess Prozor in a letter to Adrien Bovy: "You are all so terribly intelligent and cultured and bursting with the classics"[25]. Inevitably, with regard to Ramuz's own emergent style, this veneer of extreme literacy was nearly disastrous. Patronizingly perhaps, but nevertheless pertinently, Philippe Godet typifies a coldness of reception that must have humiliated Ramuz after the impetus gained from his initial publication:

Four young aesthetes from Geneva have got together to produce a "composition of Swiss-French literature." [. . .] Those four good chaps have assembled in this small volume some schoolboy essays, the printing and publication of which was not altogether necessary. There are, firstly, prose-poems from M.C.-F. Ramuz. Unfortunately, M. Ramuz takes pleasure often in speaking unintelligibly [. . .]. And to think that it is this young man of real talent who surrenders himself to such exercises![26]

Once the shock of such humiliation had passed, Ramuz absorbed the experience as a salutary lesson, noting laconically in a letter to

Bovy, "we drank too much along the banks of the lake"[27] He went on to elaborate a short time later to the same correspondent:

Aren't you like me? Don't you (you do) despise the "man of letters," his type of mind, literary banquets, the business-side of our task? Only solitude is worthwhile and a garden with lettuces that are picked in the morning with a rusty old kitchen knife; and the stem is full of a white milk which stains the fingers black.[28]

Thus, the *Pénates* experience was not entirely negative; certainly it was badly planned and concerted, and emphasized unnecessary material, but it did signal a strong mutual awareness and a determination to express French-speaking Switzerland. It was from this preliminary surge that the far more successful *Voile latine* was to be born some months later with the additional collaboration of two other young poets, Gonzague de Reynold and Henry Spiess.

For the moment, however, a mildly chastened Ramuz returned to his solitary meditation; and his diary bears almost continuous witness to a renewed yearning for perfection, which brought him to formulate in the clearest possible terms both his procedure and his artistic credo. Henceforth he would be directed only by his desire to communicate as sincerely and ingenuously as possible his vision of the world and his chosen theater. Only in that way, he declared, would he be likely to fulfill his artistic vocation;

I shall begin by doing nothing more than scrupulously painting what I have around me, as simply as possible; I do not have the right to act in any other way [. . .]. I shall subscribe to no school. I shall forget those I admire, because in thinking of them, I should lose my sincerity. I shall fear neither being naive, nor foolish, because if it is my nature to be thus, I should only avoid being so with a deceit. I shall only try to correct myself little by little. I shall place on my stage countryfolk, because it is in them that I find nature at its most pure and because they are surrounded by the sky, fields and woods. And it is possible that one day, rising by steps from life to style, from the picturesque to the linear and from immediate reality to artistic reality, I may reach those spaces where I should like to be in the light and the wind.[29]

Rarely has the nobility of authorship been expressed with greater conviction.

VII   Aline

It was in the euphoria of such a declaration that Ramuz completed, in September 1904, his first novel, *Aline*, to be published simultaneously in the following year by Perrin and Co. in Paris and Payot at Lausanne.

Although concerned with solitary human beings, isolated rather than integrated, as will be the case in later writings, from their respective communities, Ramuz already gives several indications of a burning artistic need to translate from the particular to the general, heralding his future route. Gently reminiscent of Flaubert, perhaps in *Un coeur simple* most of all, and Maupassant, *Aline* in no way suggests any imitation. The discretion, simplicity and naïveté are unmistakeably Ramuzian.

Even on the cover the little-known Vaudois writer evidenced no sign of pretension and merely termed his work "histoire" rather than "roman." And yet, just as had been the case with *Le Petit Village*, this longer work had also seen a great deal of revision and change. *Aline*, too, was originally a lengthy poem in Alexandrines:

She too had first been a poem, absolutely regular, in Alexandrines, with rhymes; I was now in the process of taking off her rhymes; she was becoming quite simple, quite modest, thanks to the prose which rid her of her artificial grace and borrowed elegance. [30]

The atmosphere of the story, understandable in view of the prevailing literary climate of Ramuz's own adolescence, is realistic, but there is more. It is a story which is doubly symbolical, the itinerary of a love in rhythm with the seasons, but also the transposition of the author's current state of mind; both Aline and Charles-Ferdinand seek an opening-out which will terminate their frustrated solitude.

The narrative begins with a brief accidental meeting between the seventeen year old country girl, Aline, and Julien Damon; it is a banal exchange but one which establishes immediately the everyday simplicity which is thereafter characteristic. The setting becomes almost idyllic with the delicious innocence of their first assignation and kiss. However, parental oposition is not long in revealing itself, and Aline's mother, Henriette, forbids any further trysts.

At this point the novel's movement is deliberately slowed down and the dragging anxiety felt by Aline, now deprived of Julien's presence, is evoked by consecutive chapters which describe laboriously a day in the life of Aline and then the same day for Julien. Eventually, a letter from Aline elicits a positive response from Julien who, however, is far less profoundly disturbed by his frustrated affection than Aline. The new rendezvous proposed in despair by the girl is welcomed by him, but his meditation on the evening ahead focuses on her likely compliance rather than on anything else—"She will do anything I wish."[31] For Aline the encounter is one of total fulfillment, her happiness sees a world born anew; but the potential tragedy is etched ever more clearly in the powerfully laconic allusion to Julien's own reaction—"Julien had slept and eaten well."[32]

Predictably, after a number of such evenings, Aline's sensitivity and emotionalism begin to disturb and stifle a Julien whose nature functions on more material lines. When on one occasion Aline bursts into tears, so terrible is her love, Julien's reaction is carefully noted by the narrator—"He saw that Aline was not made as he was. He was somewhat sorry for her."[33] Soon boredom creeps in and Julien's mind begins to turn to other, newer, pastures—it is the arrival of "le mauvais temps". In fact the onset of wintry weather offers Julien a plausible excuse for easing out of a relationship he no longer finds very stimulating, and reluctantly Aline agrees that they see each other only once a week. When Julien stops coming altogether Aline's suffering increases daily, and a vortex of dreams, nightmares, and self-examination culminates in visible evidence of her anguish in loss of weight and dreadful pallor. Then, the discovery that she is expecting a child begins the long final stage of a calvary—with clear Calvinist overtones—which takes her through Julien's rejection, her mother's anger and soon frigidity, the physical pain of a difficult childbirth, her inability to feed and the worry of a sickly child. Meanwhile "Julien . . . was in good health and glad to be alive."[34]

It is his engagement to another girl which finally dislodges Aline's already wavering reason, and in a moment of utter agony at her child's continued difficulties she smothers it and runs off into the night. She is discovered later hanging by her belt from an apple tree.

Perhaps the greatest structural weakness in a story that to this point is beautifully coherent in its *va-et-vient* between the two protagonists, always within a framework of seasonal evolution, is that it continues after Aline's death. The inconsequential final account of the funeral rites, of Henriette's loyal tending of Aline's grave, of

Julien's marriage, is difficult to understand in the light of the self-sufficiency of what precedes.

With hindsight, for us today the overriding interest of the novel is as a pointer to what was to follow. The ever-vacillating joy and despair which rack Aline so movingly are clearly born out of the uncertainty of Ramuz's own creative experience at that time. It is this translation into Vaudois village life of Ramuz's own literary soul-searching which was to characterize his writings for the next decade, certainly up to the declarations of *Adieu à beaucoup de personnages* in 1914.

Moreover, although found with greater frequency and greater impact in those novels of wider perspective which follow 1914, certain devices give early evidence of a style that is as yet embryonic. The use of a narrative present tense to include, almost parenthetically, reference to local customs is one such device, but even more effective is that contraction into the same narrative sentence of both subjective and objective point of view. We discover as early as page twelve this sentence, ". . . and then she [Henriette] waited to die in her turn, for God is just, and we mustn't go against his will,"[35] where the traditional third person narrative indicated by "she" is replaced by the clear subjectivity of the final clause which seems to shift the narration to Henriette, or at least to project a narrator who is involved to the extent of sharing simple peasant acceptance of divine authority. Both such devices were to become eminently Ramuzian.

Despite almost complete indifference in Paris, the note of Swiss critics, many of whom admittedly were friends of the author, was generally elogious. According to Gonzague de Reynold, Ramuz had composed "a strong and healthy work"[36] and Adrien Bovy went yet further, applauding *Aline* in suitably familiar tones—"At last a Swiss novel—the most beautiful or the only one (until your next)."[37] Probably the most perceptive comment came from Daniel Baud-Bovy who allows, then nuances, Ramuz's own rectification on the front cover. "It is not a novel," he concurs, but adds, "it is poetry."[38] Arguably, although labels are always invidious, there is already more of the static, contemplative, and atmospheric quality of a poem than the factual and anecdotal evolution of a novel. Ramuz himself confirms revealing:

"Peripeteia" do not interest me. The invention must not be in the subject; it must be in the way of expressing it. It is in the *tone*, in the *choice*; it is in the image; it is in the movement of the sentence; it is nowhere else.[39]

VIII *Life in Paris*

Aline and her creator had been recommended to Perrin, the Paris publishers, by the only writer whom Ramuz frequented in the capital, his compatriot and mentor Edouard Rod. It was also during those Sunday afternoons at the Rue Erlanger house of Rod in Auteuil that Ramuz encountered the Swiss painter René Auberjonois, soon to become a firm friend. Rod's often worldly gatherings of conformist journalists and literary people must have been difficult fare for the essentially taciturn Ramuz. However, although wealthy and witty, Auberjonois was clearly a kindred spirit, both "raffiné" and "primitif," and he aroused an immediate warmth in the novelist whose predilection for painters rather than writers was by now firmly established. Together they were regular visitors to the exhibitions at the galleries of Durand-Ruel, Druet and Bernheim, Roseberg, and Kahnweiler.

In the company of fellow Swiss like Fernand Chavannes, Spiess, Bovy, Blanchet, the Cingrias and an array of local painters and sculptors, they used to take their meals from 1905 onwards "chez Jouven" at the junction of the Boulevard Montparnasse and Rue Léopold-Robert, or else while away the hours at Le-Nègre-de-Toulouse, a small bar-cum-restaurant, between the Closerie des Lilas and the Rue Chevreuse, to which Edouard-Marcel Sandoz, the sculptor, had introduced them. It was there too that Ramuz rubbed shoulders with contemporary figures like Paul Fort, Moréas and Jarry.[40]

Such indeed were the events of Ramuz's life for his is one that is particularly devoid of historic incident, and the rhythm and pattern of his time in Paris changed little right up to his final departure in 1914. Undoubtedly, the single most significant action he took was to move in 1910 to the painters' milieu of the Rue Boissonade. It was there in fact, that were situated the studios of Alice Bailly and Cécile Cellier—later to become Ramuz's wife—two lady-painters that Ramuz, Bovy, and Cingria had already met briefly the previous year at an Art Exhibition in Lausanne. Alexandre Blanchet and Elizabeth Krouglicoff also had studios there and yet curiously, in the regular discussions of painting that took place, it was increasingly Ramuz the writer's opinion that was sought, savored, and usually respected. At the same time this affection for pictorial art impregnated his life and, inevitably, his own creations.

Yet, despite this medley of friends and activities, despite regular

summer sojourns in Vaud and reunions at La Belotte where the
Cingrias' mother had La Taupinière, a country home, Ramuz still
managed to accomplish a remarkable quantity of work. As well as
producing nearly a book a year, he helped to organize the new
Swiss-French rallying-point *La Voile latine*, collaborated substantially with the *Gazette de Lausanne*, the *Journal de Genève*, and the
Semaine littéraire, and even continued, only to abandon unfinished,
two more novels, some hundred or so short stories and numerous articles. But this profusion did not mean necessarily that the
moment of ultimate creativity was at hand, for the traces of that
conventional education he found so burdensome had not yet faded
totally:

I should like to attain pure sensation; to paint the complicated with very
simple words, not to describe, but to evoke, to go even sometimes, for
greater force, as far as breaking up syntax and grammar; I don't dare risk it
yet, because of the vestiges of my education, but I am moving that way.[41]

In the light of such a reservation it is not altogether surprising to
discover that the published work which succeeds *Aline* in 1906 is in
fact a renewal of the verse narrative experience just rejected in
Aline—a potentially retrogressive step just as *Les Pénates d'Argile*
had been with regard to *Le Petit Village*.

IX   La Grande Guerre du Sondrebond

At first reflection little could be further removed from the simple
charm of *Aline* than a blank verse narrative dealing with an 1847
military campaign in the Catholic cantons by federal troops to
safeguard the unity of the Helvetic Confederation. And yet, despite
the somewhat unsupported criticism of Grivel that there was a lack
of internal coherence,

the main criticism I would make, is that the tone does not go with the blank
verse [. . .]. The poetic and rhythmic intention is not sustained by the
expression, the form, in short does not correspond to the content, and
results in an impression of falsity which is soon upsetting,[42]

and despite once again a passive public, many critics, especially
those sensitive to the linguistic subtleties, again applauded a huge
creative talent beyond the deceptively ingenuous surface. Even
Grivel admitted grudgingly, "M. Ramuz's simplicity is again a very

knowledgeable one, and his naïvetés are both complex and intended."[43]

Even before opening the slim volume the delightfully direct and rustic cover designed by Auberjonois for the original Julien edition evokes the principal qualities. Thereafter the choice of an explicitly oral delivery in the guise of old Jean-Daniel permits a gentle and warm humor:

> It should also be said, to be fair,
> that they've got a very funny religion,
> They burn things during their sermons,
> they have priests who wear skirts.

> We have the Good Lord, Jesus Christ, and that's good.
> They, they also believe in the Virgin Mary
> in wooden saints, of which their churches are full
> and in paper, when it's printed,

and recurrent home-spun wisdom:

> So you see this war was soon over:
> one battle that's all.
> A good thing too, after all wars are sad.
> Fighting doesn't make anyone richer.[44]

The net result is a pleasant little work, but one that without being disastrous shows no real advance beyond *Aline*.

X *Candidate for the Prix Goncourt*

Certainly the proportions of *La Grande Guerre du Sondrebond* in no way prepared the public for the weighty volume that was to follow. The title, *Les Circonstances de la vie*, suggests quite unmistakeably a move away from a single linear story, and announces a large, sad, novel of the Naturalist type, in which detailed urban malaise replaces etched peasant destiny. It would be blind to dismiss as gratuitous coincidence the fact that Ramuz was working on an edition of Maupassant for Louis Conard at the same time as he was writing his novel, for one could scarcely conceive of a composition so admirably retrospective to the prototypes of the Prix Goncourt as envisaged by its originators. Indeed, Ramuz very nearly received the prize, and would have done so had he been French! In the end after much wrangling the award went by a single vote to a harmless, unremembered, regional novelist from Lorraine, Emile Moselly; but the publicity gained did mean that at last the Vaudois writer was established in the metropolis.

The story of *Les Circonstances de la vie* is a straightforward one, that of a weak man who ruins himself because of a woman; the setting, from the initial professional notice on Magnenat's office door, is firmly established as "petit bourgeois". Emile Magnenat, an already respected notary in a small provincial town, makes a potentially advantageous marriage to Hélène, a young, polished, reserved, and delicate girl of good family. A complication soon arrives in the inviting shape of Frieda, an attractive, German-speaking, blonde *au-pair* girl from Soleure who has come to the newlyweds to learn French. In a short while Hélène dies heartbroken, painfully aware of her husband's new interest. Magnenat envisages a new lease of life with the voluptuous "Allemande", but has to leave town because of the growing notoriety of the liaison, before he can in turn marry her. Inevitably Magnenat's career is soon in rapid decline, as he is first ruined financially by a spendthrift wife and then made cuckold when Frieda runs off with a commercial traveler.

But this brief summary obviously does not do justice to a work which embraces in considerable detail the habits, the daily life, and the attitudes of a group of society that Ramuz in fact *knew* just as intimately as the country population he chooses to express in the majority of his writings.

Primarily, it is the unreality of the bourgeoisie which is most often apparent, their Calvinist sense of guilt, the superficiality of their reactions, the checked emotion:

His first movement was to hug his wife against him, yet he didn't do it. And he would have liked to have been able to invent a sentence, a tender phrase, a gentle word, but he couldn't do that either . . .[45]

As an accurate Naturalistic portrait of members of a social stratum laboring under the unhappy fatality of their own temperament, it is extremely difficult to fault the work; but what is lacking is not knowledge of the subject, not yet literary skill, but the warmth, sympathy, and solidity which typify Ramuz's untutored villagers. The author knows them both, but one is learned and one is felt.

Published in pre-original serial form as was often the case, in *La*

Semaine littéraire on this occasion, *Les Circonstances de la vie* was nevertheless generally considered at the time to denote a development in the writer's short career, a widening of range and an increased power. Paul Seippel, for example, wrote on 16 June 1907 in the *Journal de Genève:*

It is a pleasure to follow closely the literary career of M. C.-F. Ramuz and to see the gradual development of this young talent, which acquires strength as it goes and gains, from stage to stage, in fullness, confidence and control. He has just enriched our Swiss-French literature, the hue of which is too uniformly a gentle blue, with a work of harsh reality, noble in tone, devoid of poetic sentimentality, exempt from psychological or moral dissertation. [46]

For Ramuz himself however the work seems to have been at least in part an act of exorcism, the final farewell to the Naturalistic, preeminently *literary*, school which had tended to dominate his school and university days by its impressive actuality. He nuances thus:

To renounce all species of literature although I put nothing above art—and may there be nothing higher for me than a life devoted entirely to art. [47]

There is no doubt that in the year or so which followed *Les Circonstances de la vie* Ramuz conducted unremittingly in his diary a continuous and progressive meditation on the creative process:

Style: The part of man in the *interpretation* of things. The more lofty it is, the less exact.
My ideas come from my eyes,—if I have masters, they are amongst the painters.
Disgust with the transitory, this same need for the Absolute, the Eternal— the Infinite—the absence of which makes everything seem wretched. [48]

Expressions such as these bear mute but eloquent witness to the advanced *theoretical* state of his aesthetics at this time. Key elements to which I shall return—the essential relativity of point of view, the predominance of visual allusion, and the thirst to communicate some permanence—already figure markedly in his reflections. All that was needed to stimulate the theorist towards creation was an experience sufficiently moving, sufficiently visual, and sufficiently rich in overtones of eternal authenticity to provide the living material. It was at this point, on 12 June 1907, that Payot commissioned Ramuz to produce a text for a book on Le Valais.

XI   *Le Valais*

Le Valais is that most elemental of mountainous regions situated to the east of Lake Léman, a landscape of unchanging harshness, where peaks, escarpments, glaciers, and torrents combine antagonistically to oppose man in everything he attempts. One can scarcely imagine a better microcosm of the permanently painful human condition than this rugged corner of Switzerland, and, certainly, the experience for a visitor from the gentle Vaudois plains must have been radical. The total disparity between the cantons of Vaud and Le Valais is clearly put by one Ramuz biographer, Bernard Voyenne:

Vaud is the land of man and, already, of this century: there are towns, railways, electricity, cinema. Le Valais is the elementary, raw nature, the great wild forces.[49]

And another, Maurice Zermatten, Valaisan himself, confirms the extent to which this fortuitous winter sojourn must have coincided with Ramuz's immediate novelistic needs:

Better than a retreat: the high villages presented the young writer of 1907–1908 with the example of a primitive community huddled around its church and embracing in its own destiny the destiny of the world.[50]

It was soon to become apparent that if it was Paris that had made Ramuz aware of his roots and allowed him to pursue his artistic meditation, then it was indeed Le Valais that was to give the young writer his most forceful and decisive adult experience.

The nature of the composition of *Le Village dans la montagne* as projected by Payot necessitated a vision of the mountain community common to both writer and illustrator, for the text was to be complemented by some one hundred and seventy colorplates. Ramuz's first move, therefore, was to go up to Chandolin to spend some time with Edmond Bille, the artist chosen by the publishing house. It was there that the first notes were made and that artist and author attempted to concert, rather than subordinate, their individual ap-

proaches. But it was not Chandolin that was destined to be trans-
posed by Ramuz in his text, for the advent of René Auberjonois from
Paris took Ramuz higher still, up to Lens, and it was there at the
Hôtel Bellalui that Ramuz was to spend most of the winter.

Auberjonois was a close friend of Albert Muret, another painter,
who lived in a picturesque chalet at the northern exit from the
village, and it was largely during the frequent dinners they shared at
Muret's home that the impressions gathered daily by the fresh re-
ceptiveness of Ramuz were crystallized into the basic material for
the pastoral prose poem to be published later in 1908. Writing a
long time afterwards in a book about his friend Auberjonois, Ramuz
was to stress the mutual love they shared for Le Valais, an affection
and an awareness far removed from that of the ordinary tourist or
the seeker of folklore:

They [tourists] love what particularizes it [Le Valais]: its hats, its caracos, its
neckerchiefs, its chalets, its picturesque side, all that which makes it distinctive: we, however, loved on the other hand, and still love, that which
makes it "similar," links it in primordiality with all that remains primordial
in the world.[51]

Nevertheless, despite its limited success, it was not *Le Village
dans la montagne* that was to be Ramuz's most significant publication to emerge immediately from this salutary immersion in Le
Valais. For, at the same time, he had been working on a new novel.

XII   Jean-Luc persécuté

In May 1908 Ramuz put the final dot to a work in which he
admitted a certain pride. After the unsatisfactory voguishness of his
preceding novel, *Jean-Luc persécuté* was at least a creation that,
regardless of its worth, was totally Ramuzian, and the author was
clearly happier:

What it is worth, I do not know, at least overall; what I do know, is that it is
very much mine. I had, whilst writing it, no model in my mind. I set out
with truths painfully acquired; I have set in the work an experience which is
still too brief and too unsure, but which is my own.[52]

But, even before the critics got hold of it, it became obvious to the
author that *Jean-Luc persécuté* was substantially out of step with

fashion, for it was rejected as a serial by both the *Journal de Genève* and *La Semaine littéraire*. Indeed, it never appeared in pre-original form at all and, on Edouard Rod's advice, Ramuz eventually placed it, once again, despite misgivings as to the continuing narrowness of his circle of readers, with Perrin in Paris.

After the colorless conventionality of *Les Circonstances de la vie* Ramuz returns in *Jean-Luc persécuté* to the greater simplicity of *Aline* and, once again, traces with immense discretion and dramatic force the linear path of a single destiny. But perhaps the greatest step forward is the increased stylistic coherence that brings together harsh authenticity of language, point of view, and character, and which seems to spring directly from the new mountain setting.

The structure, just as in *Aline*, offers an initial movement from happiness to tragedy and jealousy, then a rediscovery of joy before a second and this time disastrous descent.

At the beginning of the first chapter Jean-Luc Robille has been married for some two years to Christine; and they have a son, Henri, who is eleven and a half months old. One day, coming back unexpectedly to the house, Jean-Luc discovers traced in the snow the footprint evidence of his wife's infidelity with one Augustin Crettaz. After a temporary separation and despite his mother's warnings Jean-Luc returns to, but does not forgive, Christine; and they live for a time in a sort of passive discord. In the wake of a wood-cutting accident in which Jean-Luc breaks his leg, Christine's compassion and tenderness as she nurses her husband break down the barrier and with the arrival of spring—"there was happiness once more."[53]

But the return of Augustin to the neighborhood again provokes doubts which, when ultimately confirmed, incite a distraught Jean-Luc to throw out his wife. Thereafter, his inability to forget Christine and suspicions about the paternity of Henri—blond like Augustin—make him increasingly seek escape from his wretchedness in drink and abandon his son to another's care. The gradual disintegration of family, honor, and religion continues, with the pathetic death of Henri, drowned in the village pond, and then with Jean-Luc's total loss of reason. He reappears with a new but fatal vigor, convinced he is carrying his still living child, rocking and talking to an imaginary Henri. The return of Christine to the village precipitates a violent and morbid end as an utterly deranged Jean-Luc chops up an empty cradle, sets fire to Christine in a hayloft, and, after a mountain ascent of almost epic proportions, finally commits suicide by hurling himself into the gorge. The confirmation of his apotheosis, prefiguring that of Farinet and Joseph in later works, is contained in expressions such as "And he was large, on his bed, he was so very large," on the last page.

As is inevitably the case with a novelist who increasingly rejects the importance of event and incident, this factual résumé does scant justice to the quality of the work. Writing to Paul Seippel in the same month in which *Jean-Luc persécuté* was published Ramuz asserts, "As you can see this story is very short; it has no pretensions to being a novel; the plot, if one can give that name to a mere succession of events, is quite straightforward; I have sought above all a tone, and then to be brief and expressive."[54]

And yet few outside his immediate allies seemed able to recognize the quality and uniqueness of this tone. In particular Ramuz was delighted by an elogious and incisive critique penned by Robert de Traz in the November number of *La Voile latine*, and wrote to thank him: "You are *alone* (apart from a few intimate friends who do not write in newspapers) in having, in fact, *understood me.*"[55]

For the most part those very features with which Ramuz was most satisfied, those indeed on which he had spent much time and correction, were those which came in for the most severe criticism. In an age when the bourgeois novel was still undoubtedly dominant it was perhaps inevitable that the primitive instincts of Ramuz's "paysans" should appear almost feral to sophisticated commentators. Thus it was to even the usually sympathetic Gaspard Vallette, who lamented, "One cannot help regretting somewhat that M. C.-F. Ramuz only interests himself in such primitive human natures."[56]

Having consciously created his characters from those basic souls he had watched laboring all winter in the mountain wastes of Le Valais, Ramuz was entitled to feel a trifle piqued by such critical unwillingness to give more credit to his creative judgment. That he should, however, have been confronted with an even greater outcry against the language, and in particular its looseness, must have seemed inadmissibly shortsighted; for Ramuz's principal, almost entire, aim was to achieve in that area an unpolished roughness of tone which happily approximated the elementary countryman he was depicting. Moreover, even when a critic did go so far as to acknowledge the deliberation that lay beneath the superficial naïveté, he then wished it were otherwise—but without elaborating! "As for the language, I wish it were less naïve, less voluntarily naïve. It would be preferable sometimes to see a rather more coherent syntax."[57]

Similarly Jules Renard finds fault with the syntactical idiosyncrasies: ". . . if you consented to smooth over a little the unremitting harshness of your syntax. . . ."[58]

As we shall see in more detail subsequently, this blindness of most of his contemporaries to the true worth of Ramuz's original use of language, caused him to be ostracized, in particular by the Paris "morgue," for several decades. Indeed it established a tradition that may still today be the prime reason for the unwillingness of Anglo-Saxons to accord the Swiss writer more than a very cursory glance.

XIII   *Recognition and Sadness*

Nevertheless, happily, despite reviews which tended to range from lukewarm to cold, the publication of *Jean-Luc persécuté* was followed, in February 1909, by a welcome award of one thousand francs from the Schiller Foundation. The citation read:

A merit prize of one thousand francs has been awarded to the young Vaudois writer C.-F. Ramuz in Paris, whose vigorous talent has very rapidly earned him a leading place amongst the writers of French-speaking Switzerland. We have from him *Aline, Les Circonstances de la vie* and *Jean-Luc persécuté* and he only needed to be French to have won the Prix Goncourt.[59]

The award certainly came at a time when Ramuz was suffering from acute financial embarrassment, for yet another literary project proposed by that same circle of Vaudois intimates which had commenced *Les Pénates d'Argile* had foundered. The suggested *Lettre du jeudi*, a twentieth century correspondence à la Grimm and Diderot, would have required a hundred subscribers at thirty francs per annum and would have offered thirty letters of approximately eight to ten pages in that period. It was regretfully abandoned before the first one ever came to press.

But the Schiller Foundation grant did allow Ramuz to press on with both his next novel and with the putting together of *Nouvelles et morceaux*, a collection of short stories interspersed with some ten drawings by Alexandre Blanchet. On an emotional front too, it was a time of great activity. January 1910 saw Ramuz very deeply affected by the death of his mentor in Paris, Edouard Rod, to be followed only a month later by the equally tragic loss of Ramuz's own father. However, on the positive side, his correspondence begins to reveal an increasing awareness, a dawning preoccupation with Cécile Cellier, who had become very much a member of his circle of intimates.

XIV Aimé Pache

I have already emphasized that the Lens experience was a very significant one indeed, in that it gave potential substance to a stylistic shift that hitherto Ramuz had only projected in abstraction. As his close friend the composer-conductor Ernest Ansermet so pertinently observed, "I see that from our country (Vaud) to Le Valais your style—from the country to the mountains—has laid itself bare, has become harsher conforming to the décor, to the primitive, almost always instinctive, characters."[60]

Yet, curiously, for the moment, *Jean-Luc persécuté* is to remain largely an interlude, for Ramuz chooses to return to a novel he had been preparing already prior to his stay at Lens. Although it had been incubating for several years, the novel that was first to appear at the end of 1910 in the *Revue hebdomadaire* and thereafter at the Fayard publishing house in April 1911, entitled *Aimé Pache, peintre vaudois*, was in fact written in only seven months.

It is with this novel that the latent ambivalence, "poet-painter," always present in a writer whose companions and excursions were ever more likely to be associated with the world of art than of literature, becomes explicit. For, despite the title, this is a clear transposition of Ramuz's own youthful gropings as a writer, his discovery in Paris of an artistic tradition together with the nature and significance of his own country, and ultimately of his gradual reconciliation and accord with his birthright. All the autobiographical elements are present, the childhood memories, the family relationships, the Collège and Gymnase, the countryside and the metropolis. But there is far more. This is not merely a sociological documentation such as those which knew a considerable popularity at the end of the nineteenth century, but a work where the inspiration and eventual worth is more to be discovered in its exposition of the problem of artistic creation—regardless of whether one paints or writes. Ramuz himself warns of the limitations of an exaggerated admiration for surface realism, of an unwillingness or inability to probe further in a work of art: "Art begins where exactness ends; art is inexact, it must be: in that sense it is "deceit," as you say, but take care that your love of truth is not merely love of exactness. For truth and exactness are sometimes contradictory."[61]

This is no *Bildungsroman* of straightforward and simple dimensions, but the parallel, or rather interwoven, itinerary of the man and the creator, an initiation to life and to art that traverses family incomprehension, self-doubt, and moral solitude before the reluctant emergence of inspiration culminates in the miraculous beatitude of the final revelation.

I feel it is worth underlining in passing just how much this process of creativity remains relevant today, how modern in fact Ramuz's material is. From Proust onwards, the maturation of the artist has been at the very forefront of literature, but there can have been few writers who have given, or give today, such profound and sincere expression to a subject of continuing actuality as Charles-Ferdinand Ramuz.

From the very outset of *Aimé Pache, peintre vaudois* the author takes great pains to establish the veracity of his story by situating the events he intends to circumscribe very precisely—"He was born on the 20th September, 1874 to Emile Pache, justice of the peace, and Suzanne Charton, his wife." Moreover, the ubiquitous insistence on the *mot juste* in the careful descriptions of clothes, actions, and objects, superbly orchestrated in the portrait of old M. Vernet, Aimé's drawing teacher, is again unmistakeably reminiscent of the Naturalistic codes that Ramuz had been compelled to imbibe in his youth. In the novel the early childhood of the protagonist is shown to be similarly restrained and controlled, with only occasional escapes into that pastoral freedom symbolized by Rose la Folle. The particular madness of this vagabond seller of fruit and mushrooms, inevitably ostracized by respectable society, was to believe that Jesus Christ still lived on earth and frequently came to visit her. Kind and friendly to Aimé, from her ingenuous position so close to nature, she unknowingly furnished him with an education far richer and more valuable than that he was receiving at the Collège ("He was learning to see things"[62]). But Rose is more than merely Aimé's primitive mentor, she is also his poetic example; she is already, by her individuality and her creativity, the prototype of the poet, the first draft of that personage who will only attain full stature a dozen years later in the guise of Besson, the weaver of *Le Passage du poète*. Lines such as the following, fully communicating the patient naïve genius of the poet, are the essential material of both books; only the balance within the narrative will change:

She had begun once more to plait together her coronets.
Aimé used to sit on the bench. She next to him with an old blue caraco, a very frayed skirt and her hands were black like bits of dead wood.
But they were skilled and tender amongst the moss and the daisies, which they delicately brought together; they moved gently; they rose a little into the air, as if manipulating puppets, with at the ends the small pink bouquets which they tied with a string, and then from one string to another, all around the circle of osier;—a piece of work done well.[63]

It is however the twice-weekly drawing lesson with Monsieur Vernet which crystalizes both Aimé's dawning sense of vocation and his potential separation from accepted canons and tenets. In these early contacts with painting there is already an instinctively primitive approach, a personalized distinction between the artistic and the natural that is certain to become crucial. At the same time his passion for solitude and self-fulfillment reveals the inevitable interdependence of his creative and human initiations, and above all their mutual anguish. The years which follow are fraught with a continuous vacillation between joy and sadness, both in his painting and in his personal relationships. It is only at the end, traumatized by the old servant Marianne's poignant account of his mother's patient death, as she waited for a son who never came, that he begins to rediscover the fresh childhood contact with life and *things* that he had originally sensed in the company of Rose la Folle. He sees only too clearly that experiences such as Paris, and his idyll with the model Emilienne, apparent sources of inspiration, were in fact deceptive, little more ultimately than veils between Aimé and his own truth.

But the return to Vaud, although it brings renewed awareness, is not sufficient in itself to bring immediate grace as well; for this, time alone is an ally:

There is a resurrection. There are in us forces of life. They push us towards death often, but also to rise up from death, they make us die in order to live better.

He had gone out, on that evening, and had climbed up, through the woods, to a place called Les Sauges from where one dominates the whole countryside.[64]

It is there, at this high point, that the time of plenitude is announced as Aimé hears voices, just as Rose claimed to have done in earlier years. It is then that "a new sweetness stretched out over the world"[65] and that the eloquent expression "all was in harmony"[66] is underscored. Thereafter, the vision of Adrien the dragoon in uniform releases Aimé's artistic genius, and the forgiveness of Marianne attests his attainment of human communion, before the final village feast affords a symbol of that fundamental unity which is now established as the goal of both his aesthetic and spiritual itineraries: "I am moving, always, towards resemblance, it is Identity which is God."[67] This last sentence of the book could almost be exergual in the succinctness and appropriateness of its formulation.

There are few critics who would take issue with the assertion that *Aimé Pache, peintre vaudois* constituted a major step forward for the Swiss author, revealing his as yet unconfirmed capacity to evoke the general by means of the particular. Certainly this was Ramuz's intention as indicated in a letter to Edouard Rod:

I have chosen a very good general "character": I should have liked to show at the same time the man, the artist and the Vaudois—so that alongside the great particularity of a carefully indicated setting, there was the universality, so to speak, of very simple human feelings. Whence the tone.[68]

Equally certain was the very real enthusiasm of Ramuz's friends; "a very beautiful book, poignant and profound"[69] wrote Rod in reply; "it is far more than a novel, it is a beautiful poem in which nothing is banal"[70] agreed Alexandre Blanchet.

Reassured and gathering strength from such encouragement, Ramuz manifests in his journal entries of the time his new conviction and confidence:

What I am seeking is not *truth*, but *my* truth. And my truth will become their truth not by reasoning and demonstration, but by influence. An art does not explain itself, it imposes itself.[71]

Even the hostility which had long been simmering towards Ramuz's bold but unconventional disregard for accepted syntax and language rules, and which boiled over at this time, could not long dismay him; and he responded either with dignity, quoting Montesquieu, "A man who writes well, does not write as others have written, but as he writes, and it is often when speaking badly that he speaks well,"[72] or with vigor: "Simplicity is an end, not a beginning. It results from a choice in the complexity, not from a native poverty."[73]

Indeed, on one such occasion he even goes so far as to demonstrate a rare but delightful touch of humor as, in a letter to his friend Ansermet, he pretends to admit that linguistic inadequacy of which he was so fiercely accused, commencing in German and continuing in blighted French:

Ich . . . mais peut-être vous serez à même de mieux comprendre moi si j'entreprenais vous parler en langue française dans laquelle je fais exercice aussi souventement que possible est; donc je disais que moi j'avais eu à l'arrivée ici un terrible dépaysement et grande difficulté à reprendre l'habitude, mais présentement est la difficulté considérablement surmontée, et recommencé ai-je à travailler . . . .[74]

In the light of such euphoria it is not surprising that in his next novel Ramuz chose to remain extremely close to the *Aimé Pache* paradigm.

XV   Vie de Samuel Belet

Although the movement of the two novels is almost identical, there is again clear evidence in *Vie de Samuel Belet*, published in pre-original in the *Bibliothèque universelle et Revue suisse* from December 1912–April 1913, of the Vaudois novelist's increasing maturity. Albert Béguin was evidently in no doubt whatsoever as to the quality of a work which nevertheless continues to be given scant recognition by the majority of commentators: "If Ramuz had only written that book, grave and beautiful, concerted and profound, I should consider him one of the great writers of this century."[75]

Vie de Samuel Belet is the story of a life rather than an apprenticeship as was the case with *Aimé Pache*. In addition, the artistico-spiritual quest and discovery of the latter seemed to be limited to exceptional creatures, but a similar experience is now refiltered

more meaningfully through a modest workman. Once again a dis-
rupted life, involving exile and return, brings the protagonist to
eventual harmony, to an interior peace occasioned by renewed contact with the soil of his birthplace, and the accomplishment of a task
which binds his life to the beings and things around him.

The beginning of the novel is indicative both of its pedigree and of
its likely progeny: "My name is Jean-Louis-Samuel Belet, born at
Praz-Dessus, on the 24th July, 1840, of Urbain Belet, farmer, and of
Jenny Gottret, his wife, as can be seen on my papers."[76]

The above sentence not only gives the detailed biographical
background in traditional fashion, but announces a novel in the first
person singular, a simple and early version of those several devices
by which Ramuz will increasingly foster the participation of all in the
imaginative experience of the writer.

Samuel's story proceeds through a series of jobs "in service,"
before the prospect dawns under the guidance of M. Loup of his
achieving some future advancement. It is the abrupt termination of
a parallel emotional progress, in the breaking-off of his laison with
Mélanie, which causes him to abandon this promising path and to
set off into the unknown. Anecdote and detail abound, far more let it
be said than in the later writings, as Samuel and his friend Duborgel
set off on their journey to Paris. It is perhaps the moment of departure from the homeland, the changing of one's soil, of the color of
the familiar earth, that produces the most poignant pages of the
book. "You feel you are changing your nature. It seems that you are
leaving your self"[77]. Rarely has the tearing anguish of leave-taking
been more discreetly yet more forcefully communicated. Once in
Paris, although his difference from his co-workers is always obvious
to him, he is soon nevertheless, and for the first time, aware of the
larger community of Man:

I felt the distances strongly; and that the earth is not as small as I had
thought.
Yet I was already sensitive to the similarities. Despite so much diversity,
when I reflected a little, it was those above all that I saw.[78]

The experience was clearly Ramuz's own.

The growing attachment of Samuel to fundamentals does not long
coincide with Duborgel's own belief that it is rather ideas which are
of greater importance. When the latter insists that a true friend will

share his ideas concerning social revolution, the moment of separation is at hand. Samuel's subsequent journey home is substantially delayed at Vevey by his encounter with, and marriage to, a widow named Louise Chabloz. Their life together is very provincial, very banal, but interspersed with moments of great joy and sadness. Her death ends this intermediate stage and sets him off homewards once more, where he eventually reestablishes himself as assistant to Pinget the fisherman. It is this twilight of his life which brings to Samuel, physically returned to the lake, a calm acceptance of a world of which he once more feels an integral part: "I have accepted everything, I am free [. . .]. We stretch out our arms to each other, we speak to each other, we are together."[79] This shared bliss, beyond suffering and solitude, becomes almost a naïve beatitude in the final lines, as Samuel's experience is generalized to broach the exemplary:

There is no longer any difference in anything; everything fuses together, everything blends [. . .]. For everything is mixed-up, distance gone and time suppressed. There is no longer death nor life. There is no longer anything beyond this vast image of the world in which everything is contained, and nothing ever exceeds it, nothing is ever destroyed; it is one degree further, it must still be reached; but one sees rise in front of one this face, which is the face of God.[80]

It is perhaps with this paragraph that the first stage in Ramuz's literary life can be said to come to a close. For the detailed description of the destiny of an individual, culminating somewhat *accidentally* in a brief terminal apotheosis as the character becomes aware of his integral position in the world, is discontinued in the novels which follow. It is a clear-cut decision which is lucidly rationalized in the imminent theoretical writings *Adieu à beaucoup de personnages* and *L'Exemple de Cézanne*.

The accent thereafter was to shift permanently to the hitherto marginal or accidental community of Man, away from the process by which an individual gains awareness. It may have been in part the infuriating blindness of critics like M. Muret—"You are unquestionably the best of our painters of Swiss-French *manners*"[81]—which warned Ramuz that he was still too close to the Naturalistic novelists of previous years. It is more likely, however, that Romain Rolland, a recently acquired apologist of his Vaudois colleague, was sympathetic to the real reason for a change of direction at this particular point, when he cogently argued the vital significance of the Paris sojourn, coming to a close at this time, in the development of Ramuz: "It is in a foreign land that one best comes to know one's own country and oneself."[82]

CHAPTER 2

Forging an Expression

I 1913—A Watershed Year

THE year in which *Vie de Samuel Belet* was published was a
notable one in Ramuz's life, for it not only saw his marriage
take place, but was alos marked by his decision to leave Paris and to
reestablish himself in his homeland. The itinerary that had so recently been that of Aimé Pache and Samuel Belet was now to become Ramuz's own.

Ramuz had known Miss Cécile Cellier, a Neuchâteloise who had
come to Paris to study painting, for several years before their marriage early in 1913. Her studio was one of several meeting places for
that group of artists—mainly painters—who inhabited the area
around the Rue Boissonnade. Referring to her as he was always to
do as "Mademoiselle," Ramuz wrote to his friend Adrien Bovy in
these somewhat prosaic terms shortly after the wedding:

Mlle Cellier has long sleeves, a high collar, a small notary's necktie (black),
her hair pulled back from the forehead, a large bosom, a very gentle manner, somewhat dreamy, and she will no longer do any painting at all. I have
bought her a cookery book, with priced menus. She is learning to knit. She
can already do a veal-roast, a stew and beef casserole. But she is still lazy.[1]

It was in order to set up home together permanently in Switzerland
that in 1913 they resolved to abandon Paris as soon as was practica-
ble. Although the actual move was only effected in the following
year, the Paris sojourn was at an end.

It was also in 1913 that there emerged the concept of the *Cahiers
vaudois*, first a journal and then a publishing house, only to be
officially constituted the following year at Lausanne by Edmond
Gilliard and Paul Budry. However, as early as 12 March 1913,
Budry was corresponding with Ramuz in this regard, insisting to

what extent his full collaboration was essential if the project were to be successful and representative:

for a first number, the material should be unpublished, and it should be from you. [. . .] The beginning is important, and ma foi! the beginning is you. It is your fault, why are you Ramuz? It is thus; I declare here and now that a work would be neither Vaudois nor living, if you are not its originator.[2]

Seldom can there have been a more homogeneous, and yet diversely talented, group of potential collaborators than that which corresponded so energetically in the months prior to the official founding in February 1914. A musician, Ernest Ansermet; painters René Auberjonois, Henry Bischoff, Alexandre Blanchet, and Alexandre Cingria; writers Adrien Bovy, Paul Budry, Fernand Chavannes, Charles-Albert Cingria, Edmond Gilliard, Pierre-Louis Matthey, René Morax, Henri Roorda, Henri Spiess, and Ramuz himself—all concerned with the artistic communication of the sensibility of their region, for them an exemplary microcosm of the wider community of man. Although the laconic statements of the journal's statutes seem inadequate—"The *Cahiers vaudois* are not a regionalist journal. Their title merely indicates the geographic site of their birth"—Ramuz's own explanation is more substantial. I include it here, despite its length, as being revealing in respect of the purpose of the Cahiers, but also as a clear reminder of Ramuz's own direction:

The particular can only be, for us, a starting point. One only goes to the particular for fear of abstractions, which would otherwise replace the general. We mean by general, that which is living for the greatest number; the abstract is an idea, the general is an emotion. We do not want the object, to be communicated, to have first to renounce its nature. It is not a theory that is drawn from it, it is sensation. We desire it to be simple, that is universal. Few events and means devoid of complexity. Life, love, death, primitive things, things from everywhere, things from all time. But in order that that matter, that universal matter (and which is just as much African, or Chinese, or Australian as "ours") should operate effectively, it must have been felt in the extremely particular experience of our own senses, because there alone is it immediately comprehensible, immediately and deeply lived and embraced.[3]

Thus, if it was the voluntary exile in Paris which made Ramuz rediscover the wonderful truth of his own roots, it was in no small measure the collective adventure of the *Cahiers vaudois* which first allowed him to give this awareness full and adequate expression.

Yet, however, much the combined Paris-Cahiers experience crystallized for Ramuz his subject matter, it was undoubtedly an autumn pilgrimage to Aix-en-Provence, also in 1913, which hardened him in his resolve to continue to forge a style appropriate to this material, a style where the sole determining criterion would be one of *convenance*, of tone.

Fascinated, as we know, from an early age by painters and painting, Ramuz had accumulated in Paris during his systematic visiting of the Louvre's treasures three voluminous—as yet still unpublished—notebooks on the works he had seen there, including those of Cézanne. Although Ramuz did not in fact meet the Provençal master, who had died in 1906, he had assiduously attended too the 1910 retrospective Paris exhibition, and the journey to Aix was designed to renew an aesthetic lesson, at a crucial period in his own evolution.

Apart from the obvious plastic qualities of Cézanne's work, it was above all the emotion inherent in the vision that the emergent author felt was the key to the painter's greatness: "To paint according to nature, is not to copy the object, it is to realise sensations."[4]

It is one of those banal commonplaces that are nevertheless worthy of being regurgitated from time to time, that a writer producing a preface or a commentary on another artist often throws more light on himself than on his subject. It is not surprising therefore that at times Cézanne's own journey through life is seen by Ramuz in terms which are, perhaps, more apposite to his own:

He only came to himself by a return to the soil. It is thus that Cézanne alone, and by the means of this soil, raises up for us an art distinct from that of Paris, an art belonging to a race and a setting, as well as being universal.[5]

What Ramuz goes to Aix to adore in Cézanne, that ability to unite in a single artistic moment *object* and *subject*, the seen and the seer, is precisely that quality which he himself is on the point of distilling from his own experiences.

It is in the wake of these events, far more momentous in Ramuz's life than the growing clamor of war, that Ramuz rationalizes

explicitly in the inaugural text of the *Cahiers vaudois* the sources
and the foundations of his aesthetics.

II   Raison d'être

In *Raison d'être*, published in March 1914[6], Ramuz attempts to
define not only his own art, but also the credo of the artist and the
very laws of Vaudois expression. It is this intercourse between
Ramuz in particular and the artist in general which gives the work
its structure, for Ramuz's own path to date is reinterpreted as that of
all creative men. The effect of education and culture is seen as a
universal alienation of self, a dehumanizing process in which man's
essential senses are jaded, then lost, as the ability to *learn* gradually
takes command—"man had stopped seeing and feeling, because he
had begun to calculate."[7]

In this bourgeois condition, curiously deprived, man is nothing
until he can reacquire his former, primitive yet glorious, naïveté by
means of some contact with that which is basic: "this reconfrontation
with a primary reality, [. . .] this recourse to raw material, to the
object perceived without any intermediary, which might be his only
chance."[8]

It is in this respect that experience of absence and then return to
one's native soil may well prove so salutary, especially if it promotes
a resolution in the potential artist to strip himself consciously of the
trappings and veneer that society has imposed on him. It is therefore in the first instance, a new simple *physical* awareness of one's
country, devoid of conformity, tradition, or theory, that Ramuz puts
forward as a *sine qua non* of the authentic Vaudois artist:

It was necessary to abandon all that was rule, all that was teaching, all that
was tradition, all that was theory: there only remained the being of flesh, a
being who no longer knew anything, who no longer understood anything
about anything, but his senses remained with eyes to see, ears to hear. And,
finally, he found himself rich in his very impoverishment, because, in his
very core, there was always the earth, and, after so many descents, he had
finished by touching it.[9]

The communication of this new contact by the writer involves
necessarily a certain method. First, Ramuz suggests, its translation
to the sheet of paper must, if it is to be adequate, embrace both
object and subject, both the substance and the way in which it has
been received by the artist:

Respect for the object and devotion to the object, and dedication to the object only interest me for what I make of it. It is only a part of the whole, as am I, but I carry this whole in me, and it does not. It is towards this whole that I am aspiring.[10]

This is no longer the scarcely-filtered reality of late nineteenth-century literature, but a new realism, admitting and admiring the *relativity* of any fact or event.

In addition, within the Swiss-French context, the expression of such an experience by a true son of the region must perforce reflect the linguistic reality, inseparable from the reception and ultimate formulation of his experience. Ramuz rejects the justification of any stigma attached to regional dialect, yet does not advocate mere imitation; for him the local language is another "object" which, as a part of the artist's personal world, must inevitably be transposed in some way into the eventual work of art:

Our patois which has so much flavor, as well as rapidity, clarity, decisiveness, solidity (exactly those qualities which are most lacking when we write in "French"), that patois, we have only ever remembered in crude comedy or in farce, as if we were ashamed of ourselves. Yet it is to that that we shall have to return, it alone can ever serve as a model (and even there transposition must occur, for there is no art without transposition); but it alone constitutes truly a form for us, because it pre-exists, because it is defined, because it has come from the very soil.[11]

Certainly the very moving final lines of Chapter Eight of *Raison d'être* leave us in no doubt as to the position of literature in Ramuz's life, nor as to the goal of his future novelistic efforts:

But that there should exist, once, thanks to us, a book, a chapter, a mere sentence, which could only have been written here, because it is copied in its inflection from some curve of a hill, or derives its rhythm from the ebb and flow of the lake or the pebbles of a beautiful shore, somewhere perhaps between Cully and Saint Saphorin—if this little thing should see the light of day we shall feel ourselves to be exonerated.[12]

III Adieu à beaucoup de personnages

The notions set out in *Raison d'être* are continued and reapplied in even greater detail, specifically to Ramuz's own literary condition, in *Adieu à beaucoup de personnages*. This work appears both as a testament to the past, as the author situates the novels he has already written within his evolution, and as a formal announcement of intention to turn from individual destinies towards the collective fate of communities. However, if *Adieu à beaucoup de personnages* is unmistakably a landing between two stages in his writing, with the advantage of hindsight the break does not seem as radical as Ramuz himself suggests. For, even beyond the retention of similar characters and décor, the subsequent novels merely develop vigorously a tendency towards exemplarity which is at least marginal in works such as *Aimé Pache, peintre vaudois* and *Vie de Samuel Belet*. What is perhaps more important is the definition offered of his *poetic* condition, the stated conviction that poetry is both communication and communion, for it is towards the miracle of a poetic unity that his best novels will eventually lead us. This bond, in which an ingenuous closeness to basic truths and realities brings together creators as distinctive as the brickmaker, the vineyard-worker, the cowherd and the poet, is the potential source of a harmony which the troubled world of 1914 so obviously lacked:

I study the different points of the earth and everything which moves; I see that all is separate.
To what point can one converge, except towards a summit, but which is situated outside our terrestrial lives and far too high above us, unless quietly, total consciousness inhabits our torn hearts.[13]

It is this almost mystical vision of a transcendent collectivity— poetic rather than metaphysical, despite recurrent Calvinist phraseology—which will protect Ramuz in the next few years from the all too apparent divisive horror of the European holocaust.

IV   *The Great War*

The role of the 1914–1918 conflict, as it shook every section of society to its foundations, should not be underestimated in the development of any of the artists that lived through it; and certainly Ramuz is no exception. It must have seemed to confirm vividly both his adolescent rejection of the impermanence of the bourgeois world, of the precarious nature of values that are a mere legacy of a bygone age, and also his need to affirm the greater brotherhood of Man. Nor was he alone in his evocation of a collectivity beyond the individual; for there are clear links with others of his generation, with, for example, Jules Romains, despite the more patent social

preoccupations of the latter. They are conditioned by the same
climate which aspires, beyond the instant, to the intransitory: "The
state of mind that war occasions refuses anecdote, it turns away from
that which is fleeting and particular, it proceeds from cause to cause,
it aspires to the universal, it is eager for the ultimates."[14]

For Ramuz any constant in the changing, tottering world about
him is to be looked for at home, in the everyday security of the
peasant round:

So many notions that one feels are already unusable, so many outmoded
concepts! But the land here remains and the nature of this land. [. . .]
For me, more than ever, I press close to a soil, deeper than ever, I thrust
my roots into the earth.[15]

And yet, even in the comparative physical calm of the Canton of
Vaud, neither Ramuz the citizen, nor Ramuz the novelist, could
long escape the immediacy of events.

At the outbreak of the war Ramuz was not on the active list,
largely because of his several absences abroad, but was soon attached to the virtually inactive "services complémentaires." Wishing to be of some more genuine use he set off with Gonzague de
Reynold to entertain and instruct the troops with selected readings,
whilst at the same time publishing in *La Semaine littéraire* his comments on the times in a column entitled "Journal de ces temps
difficiles."

It was perhaps this continuous open reflection on war-torn man
which made the Swiss writer vividly aware of the "signs" and "prodigies" which, for the primitive imagination, provide an inevitable
introduction and accompaniment to the battle:

There was indeed, it seems, a comet, but nobody saw it. There have been
neither flaming sword, nor torrents of blood, nor abortions amongst the
women, nor apparitions like that of the Dragon or like that of the Angel, by
which it is said that wars (amongst other prodigies) are announced.
Yet the preliminary signs, for anyone who could read them, were not lacking. What must be admired is the extreme subtlety of nature, far more
"intuitive" than us.[16]

It is this very "subtlety" of nature, to which the rural inhabitants
are far more sensitive than most, particularly that mysterious capacity to reflect and even herald apocalyptic moments that will pervade

and, at times, dominate, Ramuz's fictional writings until after the
end of the war.

V   *Apocalyptic Novels*

Despite his Calvinist background and a strong Biblical influence
in his expression, it would be a misrepresentation to present Ramuz
as essentially a Christian writer. He does nevertheless believe
fiercely in the existence of inexplicable power within nature and
relates this in specific occurrences to the action of the forces of Good
and Evil. It is this mysteriously supernatural atmosphere which
pervades his work at this time, and Ramuz willingly admits that it is
the monumental stress of war which suggests, even requires, such a
tone: "War imposes a tone (everything is there)—every liberty
within this tone, none outside—war does not insist that we speak
about it, only that we speak in its way."[17]

The threat or presence of death seems to have demanded from
Ramuz a sort of apocalyptic meditation on the suffering of Man and
on the source of his present ills. The first work in which this prevails
is *Le Règne de l'Esprit malin*, for although it only appeared in its
entirety in 1917, it did appear, serialized, in the *Mercure de France*
in 1914.

Even less than elsewhere can a mere summary of the novel give
the mystico-legendary tone so reminiscent, it has been suggested, of
Claudel's *L'Annonce faite à Marie* and Péguy's *Mystères*, which after
all were of the same climate. In *Le Règne de l'Esprit malin* the initial
circumstance is scarcely unusual, certainly not disturbing. One
balmy summer evening an itinerant, Branchu, arrives in a village
which is the very picture of contentment and prosperity. He seems
at first to be heaven-sent as he enquires about the prospect of
finding work as a shoemaker, in a village that had lost one of only
two such tradesmen three days previously. Only one person, Luc,
simpleton or mystic as he may be, distrusts the new arrival and is
apprehensive. It is not long, however, before the signs begin to
appear more dramatically as the second shoemaker hangs himself,
and a fire occurs amidst strange sickness. Soon the earlier harmony
becomes general antipathy and ultimately aggression. Luc's repeated warning that these events are in some way connected with
Branchu is rejected angrily by another villager, Lhôte, who douses
Luc fatally in the village pond, effectively silencing the only lucid
voice amongst them: "It is thus that there died on the ninth day,

from pneumonia, the only one who might have seen the truth in these matters perhaps, although he did not count amongst the intelligent, but perhaps there are other eyes."[18]

A degree of respite around Christmas, owing to some unnamed benevolent influence, is followed by more crises and deaths. Branchu's real colors appear amidst prevailing sickness and lamentation, and he takes over the inn with an ever-growing number of acolytes, while the rest of the villagers hide away in abject terror of this malevolent spirit. Spring brings no release, rather an even more terrible contrast between the floods, avalanches, and anguish of those outside the inn and the prosperity and material well-being of those inside with Branchu, now the Master. After the total inadequacy of the local curate, salvation eventually comes in the very human form of little Marie Lude. She hears her acolyte-father's voice asking for help, and it is her innocence, purity, and confidence as she approaches the inn which finally destroy the diabolical influence of Branchu.

The theme is clear. This almost cosmic struggle, beyond its Biblical overtones, reflects the earthly one just beginning in 1914; it announces too the deathpangs of an ineffectual religious power and the joyful substitution of an eminently human candor and simplicity. With only minor variations the same theme—the invasion of a strange disorder into a prosaic collectively which it disturbed and yet which, after sundry peripeteia, finally returns to order—will be repeated in the novels which immediately follow.

In fact, a similar structure is apparent too in the only novel published during this period in which the overtones are historical rather than mystical. *La Guerre dans le Haut-pays* takes as its background an event from local history, which occasioned a similar ripple of fear before the tranquil waters of time washed inevitably over the disturbance. Although the currents of that particular time—equality, rights of man, republicanism, etc.—do appear in the fictional conversations, the distinction between the peasants of yesteryear and those of today is slender indeed: "Patient rather than flexible and not so much quick as stubborn, they mistrusted the vague ideas with which people tried to replace their longtime convictions."[19]

One odd, almost unique, difference from preceding and even subsequent Ramuzian novels is the conception of a character of considerable individuality in a world where collectivity is the rule. The story begins with Regent Devenoge writing a poem, and

laboring over a third-line rhyme to go with his first Alexandrine.
There is certainly rare humor, perhaps even the suggestion of a
parody of his early self, in Ramuz's presentation of the Regent's
musing:

It required, as can be understood, placing Sylvia under the invocation of
Venus, and reconciling, he said to himself, the ancient world and the modern, the seas of Greece and the mountains of Switzerland, for he had high
ambitions. But they were still, as he well realized, only ambitions; would he
ever even be of the stature to turn them into reality?[20]

The caricature is further enhanced by the Rousseauesque names
of the Regent's two children, Julie and Emile, and by his inordinate
fear of the "ministre." Undoubtedly for reasons of overall unity, this
wry and interesting figure is neither developed nor repeated.
Rather, it is the return from a French regiment of Pierre Ansermoz,
laden with firsthand experience of new social ideas, which begins
the ferment. His discussions with David Aviolat, whose links with
the lowlanders were already substantial as it was his task to go down
to collect the post, soon reveal a dangerous divison in the village,
one that polarizes around the older generation centered on David's
zealous and pious father, Josias-Emmanuel, and the younger group.
    Even in this predominantly historical drama it is not long before
the signs appear, and the imminence of war between the new low-
land ideas and the mountain traditions is announced by the venera-
ble Isaiah, a living prophet of Old Testament dimensions.
    The split between David and his father now becomes decisive and
they find themselves on different sides in the battle which is soon to
commence. Despite pangs of remorse and doubt, both with regard
to his father and to his abandoned love, Félicie, it is David who
guides the invading lowlanders up the pass towards his old village,
while, on the other side of the mountain in an almost cinemato-
graphic "crossing up," Félicie and Josias-Emmanuel independently
ascend the same peak.
    A final change of heart allows David to appear unarmed before his
erstwhile compatriots, when his father, slowly and deliberately,
shoots the son he no longer wishes to know. This emotional climax is
rapidly followed by the surrender of the commune and the lowlanders' complete victory, but with little change to normal village life
which remains as always unaltered by momentarily climactic events.

Although it intermittently reveals a similar concern for style in its frequent attempts to invoke a permanent collective village life beyond precise historical time, this is not a very satisfactory novel. Excessive historical coloring, a surfeit of anecdote and a wavering between the historical, the epic, and the mystical, damage a work that is perhaps best understood as yet another corner of the "apocalyptic" parenthesis in Ramuz's novelistic evolution.

After *La Guerre dans le Haut-pays* Ramuz's next four novels—*La Guérison des maladies* (1917), *Les Signes parmi nous* (1919), *Terre du ciel* (1921), *Présence de la mort* (1922)—all reveal a constant thematic formula which revives almost exactly that first found in *Le Règne de l'Esprit malin*. In each case the strange, unnatural plight of the villagers, faced with signs and events they can barely interpret, let alone counteract, is only resolved finally by the unintentionally redemptive quality of some naïve human action, as Marie Lude is replaced by Marie Grin or by yet another. Because of this repetitiveness, and also in the light of Ramuz's later, mature works where his primary concern for creative man is no longer clouded by the *apparent* importance of contemporary world events, I shall not dwell further on these novels which are however of some interest as documentary evidence of the gradual coming together of that style which I shall only analyze in detail with regard to the great novels. Let us simply note at this point that there occur increasingly, but still spasmodically, devices such as Biblical language and reference, fragmentation of point of view, multiplicity of tense, reduction of incident, all of which will be recognized as fundamental to his ultimate expression.

Therefore, although it may be somewhat of an impoverishment, it is not altogether unreasonable, and certainly more illuminating, taking into account the manifestos of this time, to consider the period from 1913 up to the notable publication of *Le Passage du poète* in 1923 as essentially an extended exercise in style, obscured and confused at times by the secular Armageddon which so ravaged those years.

VI   *The Influence of Igor Stravinsky*

It was during the war years too that Ramuz enjoyed the human relationship that may well have been the most meaningful within his artistic development, and one that demands our attention at this point. Igor Stravinsky was first introduced to the Vaudois writer by Ramuz's longtime friend Ernest Ansermet in the autumn of 1915. The Russian composer was then living at Montreux and already receptive to the Swiss landscape when he made that fateful journey along the edge of the lake to Treytorrens, between Cully and Rivaz. Certainly Ramuz himself was never in doubt as to the role played by the countryside around them in that first warm encounter—"We came to know each other in front of things and through things".[21] This common attachment to the everyday objects around them provided the starting point for a communication that was to bring home to Ramuz in very concrete personal fashion that on which he had reflected and theorized so long—the universal brotherhood of man. The Vaudois experience was now generalized within his own life.

Ramuz's admiration for the Russian was immediate and lasting; the latter assumed for the Swiss-French novelist the living dimensions of the "homme complet," the very prototype of his poet-to-be:

that is to say refined and at the same time primitive, someone who is sensitive to all the complexities, but also to that which is elementary, capable of the most elaborate mental combinations and at the same time of the most spontaneous and direct reactions;—as is right, for one must be both untutored and civilized; one must not only be a primitive, but one must *also* be a primitive.[22]

Soon Stravinsky was living at Morges, while Ramuz was nearby, not far from Lausanne. Frequent telephone calls and reciprocal visits took even firmer shape when they began to collaborate, as Ramuz translated into French for his new companion the Russian text of first *Renard* and then *Noces*. It was this day-to-day working contact which provided Ramuz with the necessary confirmation that his own artistic itinerary, not yet consecrated by a truly great work, was nevertheless the right one. He wrote to Stravinsky, "You have freed me from my doubts and my scruples; you have taught me, by being yourself, to be myself."[23]

It was also Stravinsky who stimulated Ramuz to affirm unequivocally that only utter authenticity in man was a positive and enduring force:

You have given me the example of spontaneity, which is that which we most need in this country, where natures are so bent on analyzing, judging, confronting each other that they finish by no longer acting, nor even reacting at all.[24]

But above all it was undoubtedly this first direct experience for Ramuz, not of mere friendship, but of total human communion, which was the most glorious aspect of their association. Beyond the insistent clamor of war, beyond the frustrations of his material and artistic life, Ramuz now saw, knew, and lived *Man*:

Everything in life had found for a moment its solution, and satisfying at the same time body, senses, feelings, soul, mind, intelligence: then one was above the times. There was only now one time to which one had returned and which had neither beginning nor end: that of before the Tower of Babel, before the confusion of tongues, letting us glimpse even further back the Great Lost Garden of unity: unity between men, the interior unity of each of them. And there was no longer any space, that is a space which separates.[25]

These were in Ramuz's life days of great purity and plenitude, and they inevitably colored his vision of contemporary events. Even the news of the Russian revolution becomes in *Le Grand Printemps* a corroboration of the immense importance of his own current experience. Rejecting Goethe's notion of the "poètemage," Ramuz interprets the 1917 revolution as the coming of the collectivity, the enthronement of the community and of the true poet who embraces it in his song:

Not the song of a single person: but the song of all together. Not the poet-individual, but the poet-nation. Not a poetry of words alone, but a poetry of all existence.[26]

This classification of the poet's nature and function was given effective and visible force by the happy decision of Ramuz and Stravinsky to compose jointly an original work.

Although the result *is* remarkable, it would be foolish to suggest some insistent common voice demanding release; for the project from the outset was born of circumstances. Most theaters and concert halls, certainly the Russian Ballet, were inactive because of the war; and Ramuz himself admitted repeatedly in his correspondence how difficult it was to find publishing openings. Hence the idea of collaborating in something simple that could be put on anywhere, an unsophisticated, mobile spectacle, appropriate to any town or village, with extremely limited instruments, actions, décor, etc.— this was to become the celebrated *Histoire du soldat.*

So closely interwoven were their respective responsibilities in this creation that Ramuz, the writer, drew largely on Russian folklore, while Stravinsky, the composer, felt compelled to include trombone and "cornet à pistons," both so popular in the local Vaudois fanfares. With close friends René Auberjonois and Ernest Ansermet in charge of décor and musical direction respectively, the result was as homogeneous a spectacle of multiple authorship as could be imagined.

The story of *Histoire du soldat* tells of a soldier on leave who sells his violin to the Devil. The book that the soldier receives in return foretells events and allows the soldier to amass great riches, but no happiness. In a brief interlude the soldier does escape the enmeshment of his pact with the Devil and cures an ailing Princess with the music from his repossessed violin. But it is the Devil who triumphs in the final scene as the soldier follows him off. Since that first production in Lausanne on 29 September 1918 the *Histoire du soldat* has enchanted audiences in nearly every country in the world. Its continued success suggests that, gloomy though the spectacle's ending may appear at first sight, the real message would seem rather to lie in the soldier's renunciation of the false joy of wealth, and in his capacity to dispense joy and happiness by his art with the violin. Beyond his essential mortality, the soldier's tale is therefore, rather than any prophecy of doom, an early hymn to the miracle of human creativity.

VII   *Prior to* Le Passage du poète

Although Stravinsky's international status took him away in later years, this period of contact was sufficient to allow Ramuz to crystallize definitively his artistic concepts and to conclude his series of technical "drafts." By the time that the Russian moved on Ramuz was in full possession of his powers and ready to attempt his first great work, *Le Passage du poète*—in many ways an eloquent testimony to, and reformulation of, the Stravinsky encounter.

However, before looking at that work in detail, it is necessary at least to catalog the other signposts that emerge from the years so dominated by Stravinsky.

At the end of 1915, the year when the two artists first met, Ramuz was engaged in a series of some ten lectures at the Lausanne Conservatory on *Les Grands Moments du XIXe siècle*. This highly personalized view of the period is liberally sprinkled with observations which throw fascinating light on his apparent subject. He admits, for example, to being particularly fond of Balzac, and defends him with not altogether surprising passion against those who have accused the author of *La Comédie humaine* of poor writing:

An author writes well when he expresses himself in his entirety; to write well, it is for him to realize himself completely, such as he is, with what are called his faults, and with what are called his qualities.[27]

Similarly, his conclusions about the nature of the increasing importance of the everyday object through the nineteenth century, as he invokes Delacroix, Corot, Manet, Berlioz, Wagner, and Debussy, are not without personal connotation: "Not that the object in any case is essential in itself; it is essential only through the emotion that is drawn from it."[28]

It is this emotional attachment to things about him which generates, contemporaneously, that most haunting hymn to his daily surroundings, the very beautiful *Chant de notre Rhône*, published in 1920. The ingenuous thrill of belonging to a burgeoning countryside, washed through by this living proof of continuity, is the common lot of artist and peasant. It is the wonder and certainty of universal participation in the external world, the harmony of all natural life, which engender the strikingly lyrical tone—"O book of blood-relationships, great book of living flesh, you must be read to the very end".[29]

But Ramuz's aspirations from the very beginning have always been almost entirely novelistic. Since 1914, amidst the European turmoil, his fiction as we have seen was dominated by a sort of semi-pagan mysticism, with just the suggestion of a belief in the almost divine power of poetry. As the noise of battle dwindles and as the lessons of Cézanne and Stravinsky become absorbed, it is chiefly this transcendental dimension in aesthetic creation which comes to the fore. The prodigies and the supernatural disappear to leave only the spontaneously magical transmutation of vulgar reality under the benevolent influence of the poet-peasant.

The key text, a slim but vital credo, is entitled unmistakably

"Antipoètique" and appeared for the first time as one of a collection of short pieces grouped together as *Salutation paysanne,* published in 1921:

Poetry is only made with that which is antipoetical.
Music is only made with that which is antimusical.
Our real friends are the craftsmen, and not those called artists.
"Art," we know what it is: it's something grafted onto something already grafted.
Well, as all who do grafting know, you only graft onto an original.
You only graft onto an original plant; that's how we graft.[30]

One could scarcely imagine a more evident rejection of bourgeois poetic tradition, indeed of any art founded on anything other than total originality; and certainly the short pieces which make up the remaining pages of *Salutation paysanne* are remarkable for their freshness and vigor.

Typical is the title piece in which a peasant greets with unaffected enthusiasm the world about him, seen in new splendor as he emerges from a wood after a tryst with his loved one: "Hello! hello who? hello everything . . . Hello, tree, hello, the fields, hello, the sky, everything living."[31]

His transparent and infectious emotion provokes in the world a new "expansion", a re-creation. As he remembers the past few hours, his experience of love is once again an active force, generating a new and ever mobile space:

Where do I finish, and where does she begin?
He lays down once again this strong body [Louise's]
in front of him, that was held, that was known,
that was visited all over as are now the beauties
of the earth;—so that hill, down there, is it not rather her shoulder? and is that yet another hill,
the beautiful shoulder over there?[32]

Obviously, in purely scientific terms it is the immediacy of external perception which Ramuz is communicating here, but what is implicit is that a naïve contact with the world—such as that here of the peasant, or else of Simon in *Gare* and Frédéric the mole-catcher later in the collection—is fundamentally a creative experience, a poetic experience.

It is worthy of note that the vignettes of *Salutation paysanne* reveal, in scattered distribution, the full range of devices that will recur in more concentrated and coherent form in *Le Passage du poète* and the novels of maturity—in particular the almost static narrative, devoid of anecdote, and impregnated with present participles, existential verbs, and nominal constructions. Predictably, in a career which had hitherto been characterized by halting self-doubt, although Ramuz seemed at this point in time to be equipped fully to produce the first of a numbr of significant works, there was to be one more slight falter before the marvelous *Passage du poète*.

Perhaps because it is more accessible and less subtle *La Séparation des races* has been dealt with rather kindly by the critics over the years, in view of its very obvious weaknesses. It is a somber drama with, as the title indicates, an ultrasimple, over-rigid, structure of balanced tableaux, directly reflecting the straightforward division, Bernese v. Valaisans, blonds v. browns, protestants v. papists, but with little to commend it otherwise. The gamut of expression is infinitely more restricted than will be the case in subsequent writings, or even than had been heralded in recent works. Undeniably, the alternating tableaux do fragment the narrative and do create a form of stasis, but it is a particularly unambitious attempt by comparison with that which was to follow a year later. The intentions are clear, the realization is still to come.

VIII   Le Passage du poète

If we were to seek from Ramuz's considerable number of published works one which was most liable to survive the vagaries of fortune and fashion in centuries to come, it might well be the softly idyllic *Passage du poète*. This short novel was first announced in September 1923 when Ramuz wrote of it, in his normal laconic manner, to his friend Raoul Grosjean, admitting, "I am quite fond of it."[33] In its revelation of a communion beyond solitude, demonstrated and prepared by the poet-peasant, it provides an uncluttered key to the author's vision of the world; in its utterly stripped narrative and resolutely neutralized setting it manifests clearly the stylistic qualities that Ramuz had been studiously forging since his earliest years.

The arrival of Besson, the traveling basket-weaver, at an unnamed village at the beginning of the book is presented unmistakably as an illumination. Even on the grayest of days his advent is remarkable: "suddenly there was in all this grayness something which gave light, producing brilliant color."[34]

The usually mistrustful and reticent villagers react unforeseeably, and are happy to communicate their fears, anxieties, and hopes to the new arrival. Even the sparrows in the planetrees of the square where Besson sets up business are at ease and undisturbed by the skilled and reassuring movements of the basket-weaver, as his supple fingers surge to and fro, speaking their own simple language. As the days go by, whenever he works and wherever he goes, Besson brings light:

He takes a step, he takes a second step at the bottom of this final slope that he is climbing and where there is only poor gray grass and fog; but drives the fog from him with his arms, and then it is higher up that he looks [. . .]. He began to say to that sky: become blue; he drives away the fog with his arms, he thrusts it backwards. He said to the sun: arise![35]

Although this "creation" begs the analogy with Genesis, what Ramuz in fact chooses to reiterate on each page—far from any religious association—is rather the identity of peasant and poet: "It [the craft of the basket-weaver] is like when one writes a first beautiful line of words on the page, because it is at the top that one begins to write."[36]

If the poet is the person who *expresses* most eloquently the joy of common manhood, the peasant too, by the creative quality inherent in his manual labor, is unknowingly an eternal fundamental prototype. Thus Bovard, conscious of a new fraternity, is intended to be representative:

Being of those who have never changed, being faithful,—whilst the conductor is heard to shout: ready!—being that man with an unchanging job of work, being that man who is on the same point of the earth from the beginning of the year to the end, from the beginning of life to the end, and motionless as everything passes, everything moves, everything changes.[37]

Indeed, in the final count, there is no important distinction between poet and peasant, the former's capacity to create is not essentially different from that of the peasant. The poet "is simply a man amongst men, a man like other men."[38]

The narrative continues through a series of encounters and visits, mere immobile scenes, coordinate rather than consecutive, in which the seed of renewal is ever more widely propagated, with, meaningfully, the birds and the children as certainly not the least receptive spirits to Besson's message. The new global awareness of a collectivity beyond the individual, of a common and naïve relationship to the world around us, is acknowledged initially by Calamin, whose perspicacity, sharpened by alcohol, is nevertheless valid: "There was him, there was me, there was you, but now it is beginning to be arranged, do you see, because there is no longer me, nor him, nor you. [. . .] In truth, all together."[39]

The message is confirmed in more precise and sober terms in the description of the three men who leave the village café arm in arm: "it is an identity of bodies, there is no longer any difference and it is the communication of hearts and they are no longer separated."[40]

The consecration of this fresh sense of harmony and belonging comes in the festival at the end of the book, as the village community is swallowed up in the larger agglomeration of several villages. The poet's work is done and so Besson leaves the contentment of the celebrations, setting off inevitably towards new work, new illumination:

before him is the night of that which is not yet; against which he advances, and goes on advancing, and against that great mass of shadow because there the forests begin: so he himself disappears, and his person disappears, going still further into nothingness, so that something may be.[41]

Rejecting totally all forms of aestheticism Ramuz sets out in the text of *Le Passage du poète*, as rarely had been done before, the remarkable universality of the truly poetic experience, uniting as it does all those who retain, in however simple a form, an authentic creativity. But, if the experience is common, it is the poet who in exercising his "métier" through his style gives suitable voice to the experience. It is this expression, the techniques by which Ramuz the poet will now finally inform his vision in all its splendor, which I shall attempt to define in the following chapter.

CHAPTER 3

The Mature Works

I A Time of Consecration

SEVERAL artists of the early years of this century were directed in their work by a desire to express adequately that human quality which Gide termed "le natif" and Unamuno "lo original." Ramuz himself falls within this group; indeed, I would even contend that in the decade which followed *Le Passage du poète* he completed at least three remarkable novels which entitle him to be considered as its greatest representative. *La Grande Peur dans la montagne* (1926), *Farinet ou la fausse monnaie* (1932), and *Derborence* (1934), all bear witness to that fundamental authenticity which is man's most primitive and enduring characteristic, and it is on these three novels that Ramuz's glory rests.

Not that there were not other narratives of considerable merit during this same period; for *L'Amour du monde*, *La Beauté sur la terre*, *Adam et Eve*, and *Le Garçon savoyard*, all have their admirers. Yet, although they reflect the same vision, they lack the formidably severe coherence of the other three, in which little more than an unsophisticated presence in a mountain setting is sufficient "plot." The introduction of some strange catalyst, for example, the bewitching silver cinema-screen in *L'Amour du monde*, Juliette the exotic foreigner in *La Beauté sur la terre*, the tightrope artist in *Le Garçon savoyard*, to activate that which is spontaneously combustible in those novels situated on a mountainside, seems to disrupt and distort the internal harmony. In addition, it is in the works placed predominantly in the vicinity of the lakeside, where the quality of light is rendered even more compelling by the reflection of the water, that the pictorial tendencies of the author are most pronounced. The result of these two circumstances is a group of novels contemporaneous to the three *chefs d'oeuvre*, but which, despite

68

passages of undeniable beauty, are somewhat less perfect in construction.

This period of maturity was also a time of relative consecration for Ramuz whose name, since his launching by Grasset in 1924, was increasingly to be discovered at the center of informed literary discussion. Admission, along with writers like Alain, Max Jacob, Valéry Larbaud, Duhamel, to the exclusive group which had been interviewed in the prestigious series "Une heure avec Frédéric Lefèvre"[1], was soon followed in 1926 by the publication of a first collective homage in *Cahiers de la Quinzaine* with elogious contributions by Paul Claudel, Henri Ghéon, Daniel Halévy, Jacques Maritain, Henri Pourrat, and Henry Poulaille.[2] Still largely unloved by the general public, Ramuz had now become to the more perceptive of the critics a notable contemporary figure. Certainly the enthusiasm displayed by Henri Barbusse in *L'Humanité*—"le meilleur écrivain actuel"[3]—was no longer regarded as outrageous. It was in 1926 too, the year that saw the wealthy and benevolent industrialist Henri Mermod become Ramuz's publisher and friend, that Jean Paulhan opened the pages of the *Nouvelle revue française* to the Vaudois poet. Thereafter, the honors accumulated, with the landmark of the Grand Prix Romand in 1928 being crowned finally on 18 October 1936 by the award of the Schiller Foundation Prize.

It is these years, then, between the publication of the prophetic *Passage du poète* and the tangible recognition of 1936 that are illuminated by the perfect integration of Ramuz's novelistic art in all its fullness. It is, therefore, to a definitive statement of the nature of this art, at its apogee, that we shall now turn ourselves, with particular reference to those three novels already singled out as most worthy. In the preceding pages I have repeatedly referred to the gradual emergence of sundry aesthetic landmarks; however the scope of the present study allows only a detailed *synchronic* analysis of the author's art, not an exhaustive examination of an evolution. Having carefully traced the thematic development of the Swiss writer through the variations in plot in each of the early novels, up to a clear exposition in *Le Passage du poète*, it is now my intention to abandon such a procedure, which will take us no further into Ramuz's world, and to focus our attention on the wonderful intricacy and coherence of Ramuzian style in its best formulations.

La Grande Peur dans la montagne, the first chronologically, relates how amidst great debate the decision was finally taken by a village council to use once more, as a summer pasture, the ill-reputed Sasseneire high on the mountainside. With four other companions, Joseph, Barthélemy, and the enigmatic Clou commence their activities, but are soon disturbed by strange nocturnal activity. When the herd is struck down with fatal sickness, the pasturage is forcibly quarantined by the fearful villagers; events accelerate relentlessly towards the final avalanche which destroys all those who dared to confront the mysterious and hostile powers of the mountainside.

In a somewhat different vein *Farinet* presents a symbolic hero who, although admired for his honesty by his fellow countrymen, is in fact in the eyes of "society" merely a counterfeiter. Having escaped into comparative safety high in the mountains, he refuses to stop minting coins which are purer and more authentic than those issued by officialdom. Increasingly, however, his life becomes a series of skirmishes with outraged "Justice"; and he ultimately dies in the cause of uncompromising truth.

Derborence returns to an event similar to that which was described in the climax of *La Grande Peur dans la montagne* and recounts an eighteenth century rockfall which buried a village's summer cowherds in the pasturage of Derborence. After nearly two months one of the unfortunate interred, Antoine, emerges and causes terror in a village which can no longer admit him as a living creature, only as a malevolent specter. It is Thérèse, Antoine's wife, who eventually reincorporates this "revenant" into the village by her demonstration of love as she reveals with an embrace his unaltered humanness.

But, beyond their story lines, distinctive even in their common simplicity, there is a consistency and a homogeneity in the way in which the subject is informed which points unmistakably to the now mature creator.

II *Narrative Stasis*

It is banal to observe that since the last quarter of the nineteenth century the technique of the novel in much of Western Europe constitutes primarily an investigation and an implementation of the notion of time. It is less banal, however, to contend that, in this respect, no writer during or since that period has successfully utilized such an extraordinary range of narrative devices as Ramuz in his determination to transpose stylistically his vision of a human permanence beyond the peripeteia of current events.

In the traditional novel temporal development was chronologically ordered, linked to a rationalistic system within a stable and coherent universe. The fundamental rule of narrative mode was rigorously respected: from the initial situation the action advanced in regular and consecutive fashion to its eventual conclusion. However, the advent of Flaubert heralded the imminence of crisis and, increasingly, conventional construction of plot was challenged until Alfred Jarry in *L'Amour absolu* rejected provocatively all novelistic principles of causality and dependence. As the exigencies of plot became less and less constraining, authors like Joyce, Gide, and Woolf chose in their turn to explode the temporal form of the novel: it is this invertebrate novel of the twentieth century, where "pattern" replaces action, which is evoked by Louis Cazamian when he writes of "this decadence of the story line in the most interesting and most modern novelists, in favor of what the Anglo-Saxons, in line with Henry James, call the 'pattern'."[4]

While avoiding a diachronic interpretation such as that of Cazamian, Ramuz, too, acknowledges a basic dichotomy in creative approach and distinguishes between two fundamental aesthetic attitudes to the writing of a novel. For him "invention" and "imagination" are widely divergent faculties:

I have no invention; I only have imagination. These two faculties which have nothing in common and are even deliberately contradictory are too often confused [. . .].
Invention is event, it thrives on event, delights in weaving a plot, in complicating, in diversifying the peripeteia, and in only unravelling once their possibilities have been exhausted. Invention is dynamic, [. . .] imagination, on the other hand, is contemplative. In that long succession of events where invention chooses to combine the peripeteia, it chooses one aspect which is immobilized; whereas invention accelerates, imagination fixes and restrains.[5]

Ramuz suggests that fact and event are the children of invention and produce conventional novelistic movement forwards, whereas, in direct contrast, imagination imposes a slower, more reflective rhythm. It is evident that Ramuz considers the imagination to be the generative source of the novel as he understands it, but he is not

unaware that the operative term 'roman' has now become
stereotyped by its association with a certain sort of novel: "The word
"novel" is unfortunate; it is ugly now, it has been dragged about
everywhere . . . the best would be to find another name [. . .] the
novel must be a poem."[6]

The invocation of the word "poème" is extremely significant, for it
implies already the distinctive time element which we wish to present as characteristic of Ramuz's mature writings. Clearly, in our
world of shifting terminology, it would be naïve to speak of novel or
poem as an absolute, exclusive, genre; nevertheless the substitution
of imagination for invention does tend to result in a static quality
which denies novelistic time—Sartre's "devenir romanesque"—and
is indeed similar to that of poetry. Thus, from a temporal point of
view, the essential difference between a poem and a novel opposes
the immobility of the former to the movement of the latter, in that
the poet seeks to petrify time whereas the novelist formulates an
evolution. For the poet the thread of a story, vital to the novelist, is
at most incidental. The novels of C.-F. Ramuz could not survive
without a skeleton plot, the absence of which would plunge the
reader into either incomprehension or boredom, but the essentially
poetic objective of the writer creates a tension where various
techniques resist normal narrative development. It is my intention
to examine on three levels the factors which contribute to this condition which I shall term stasis: I shall consider, first, the fragmentation of traditionally continuous and ordered narrative, second, its
deceleration and, finally, its virtual immobilization.

III   *Fragmentation*

Refusing any comfortable unilinear progression, Ramuz's temporality requires from the accomplice reader a series of disconcerting
leaps out of the accepted past-present-future continuum. Indicative
of the several techniques employed, the flashback, a narrative
movement in reverse, towards the past, offers an obvious contrast
with the normal sequence of events. For example, in *La Grande
Peur dans la montagne,* during the ceremonial ascent to the ill-fated
Alpine pasture, a flashback serves to explain how Victorine and
Joseph come to be at the end of the procession:

After them (the animals) came the third mule, carrying the provisions, that
is cheese, dried meat and bread for three weeks, it's Joseph who was with

the third mule, and with Joseph was Victorine. They found themselves at the end of the procession, because Joseph had said: "we'll be quieter", then he said: "Climb on, he's strong." It was a big red mule, four years old. And she, "Do you know how much I weigh?"—"That doesn't matter, climb on anyway . . ."
She had climbed up on to the mule; then they had left a little space between the column and themselves; there was then, after the animals, a stretch of path without anyone, then they came, at the end of the procession with the big red mule. The animals had just entered the forest.

Après elles (les bêtes du troupeau), venait le troisième mulet, portant, lui, les provisions, c'est-à-dire du fromage, de la viande séchée et du pain pour trois semaines, c'est Joseph qui était avec le troisième mulet, et avec Joseph était Victorine. Ils se trouvèrent fermer la marche, parce que Joseph avait dit: "on sera plus tranquilles," puis il a dit: "Monte seulement dessus, il est solide." C'était un gros mulet rouge de quatre ans. Et elle: "Sais-tu combien je pèse?"—"Ça ne fait rien, monte toujours . . ."
Elle était montée sur le mulet; ensuite ils avaient laissé un petit espace venir se mettre entre la colonne et eux; il y avait donc, après le troupeau, un bout de chemin sans personne, puis eux venaient, fermant la marche avec le gros mulet rouge. Le troupeau venait d'entrer dans la forêt.[7]

In this passage the principal tenses which communicate the narrator's point of view are the past historic (l. 4) and the imperfect (l.9). Between these two verbs the explanatory flashback is introduced by "parce que" and its anteriority is attested by the appropriate change in tense. This insertion of Joseph and Victorine's past dialogue, which interrupts momentarily the narrative advance, constitutes a short detour between the expression "fermer la marche" and the subsequent derived form "fermant la marche." The almost identical vocabulary ensures that the flashback is as formally isolated as if it were between brackets.

A flashback may function on two levels. In the second chapter of *Farinet* the reader is drawn back into the past as the hero recalls his initial escape from prison; but, in the process of remembering, Farinet returns by a further flashback to an even more distant past, to the period where he first met at Mièges his mentor Sage. The continuity is doubly violated.

The temporal construction of *Derborence*, considered globally, reveals not only instances similar to those already mentioned, but other notable reversals of chronology. Since the story is situated two centuries ago, the night of the avalanche—June twenty-second—

with which the description commences is already far removed from the moment of narration. Then, in the second chapter, the reader discovers himself briefly in the present of the narrator before being abruptly returned to a habitual past which evokes the significance of June fifteenth, day of the traditional journey to summer pastures. This complexity continues throughout the book and underlines the anti-linearity already deduced from our initial glance at *Farinet* and *La Grande Peur dans la montagne*.

It is perhaps worth making reference once again at this point to the value of *Le Passage du poète* as an embryo. For prior to the structure of a whole work, *Derborence*, being predominantly based on a flashback, there is in that book the occurrence of this technique, microscopic in size, but without being any the less indicative:

— If we could ask you . . .
    Besson:
— You can.
    They said
— Where do you come from?
— From more or less everywhere
    There was already no more time, now there was no more space:
— From America?
— From America
    Relaxed, holding his glass, which he empties slowly looking at you quietly from beneath his brow as it inclines forward underneath his hat; then his beard moved back and he raised his glass again.
— Why not?
    Because someone had said
— From China?
    And they laugh, and he laughs too.[8]

In this extract the enigmatic reply ("Why not?") which precedes the question ("From China?") reverses the normal order and emphasizes the importance of another sentence—"There was already no more time." Once again, textually, the effect precedes the cause; and logical temporal progression is visibly disturbed by the prolepsis.

Another means by which Ramuz breaks up the narrative is that of the parenthetic expression. The interpolation of such phrases, indeed sometimes entire passages, which furnish supplementary information tends momentarily to deflect the reader's attention from the main subject matter. In this way the elucidation of a regionalist term may occasion a pause, however brief, in the unfolding of the story. For example, in *La Grande Peur dans la montagne* the word "bottilles" is followed by its definition in parentheses: "They left at four in the morning with their lanterns and some provisions, not to mention one or two 'bottilles' of muscatel (which are small flat barrels made of larch-wood, about a pot or a litre and a half in capacity."[9]

Similarly, in *Farinet* the meaning of "galères" is given parenthetically: "For a long time he remained motionless, having to make certain first that all was quiet in the 'galères' building (which is the local name for prison)."[10]

Sometimes these pieces of information, which contribute nothing to the development of the plot, are quite considerable and interpose a lengthy interval between two sections of the narrative proper. There is a typical such passage in *Derborence:*

It was an hour later that the stretcher appeared.
They sometimes bring down on a stretcher an injured goat, the people from the chalets up there, when a goat for example, has torn a horn in a fight, or else broken its leg. They tie it onto a stretcher. They cover it with an old piece of cheese-cloth. One of the men grasps the front of the stretcher, another grasps the back. [. . .]
They were indeed carrying a stretcher, that morning, and it was indeed covered with a cheese-cloth, but it was not a goat that was lying on top.[11]

While in the process of relating the descent of the stretcher on which lies the body of Barthélemy, victim of the mountain's malevolence, the narrator interrupts the action in order to introduce some generalizations concerning the usage of such equipment. Just as the parentheses are materially absent in the above extract, so they may be replaced by an expression like "c'est-à-dire" which fulfills the same disruptive and anti–narrative function.

If the techniques so far examined remained isolated cases, one could perhaps contend that their aim was, on the contrary, perfectly normal novelistic practice; one could suggest that the plot benefits from these delays in narrative progress, that the author is merely accumulating conventional moments of suspense in order to intensify the dramatic quality of what follows. It is with much justification that Madame Guers-Villate writes in her valuable book on Ramuz: "The repetition of a date which punctuates the story is in *La Grande Peur* a means of creating an atmosphere heavy with imminent fatality. [. . .] A similar device is to be found in *Derborence*."[12]

We could even add to the two examples of Madame Guers-Villate *Farinet*, where the minutely detailed description of a room twice arrests the course of events and creates periods of expectation.[13] In a writer more consistently orthodox, one might indeed be tempted to assess such instances as nothing more than the creation of suspense; however, in a writer whose declared aesthetic goal is antitraditional and essentially poetic, an interpretation which emphasizes primarily willful fragmentation of the narrative—though less conformist—is more likely to be valid, especially when confirmed by other convergent techniques.

IV *Deceleration*

As we have already suggested, an area of Ramuz's writing which long confused critics was the extreme originality of the nonliterary language used in the narrative itself, a language which is often identical to that of the dialogue. Today, however, the narrator in Ramuz's novels is beginning to be recognized as a sort of collective consciousness of the village who necessarily speaks the same language as those observed. Without analyzing the structural corollary which is our present preoccupation, Madame Guers-Villate acknowledges, in both narrative and conversation, the heaviness and slowness which typify the intellectual process of the countryman:

Ramuz seeks neither elegance nor consciseness, for he wishes the entire story—the narrative as well as the conversations—to have the heaviness of oral language where words form one by one, following the intimate rhythm of thought which makes its way, turns back, insists, and follows an emotive rather than a logical development.[14]

In Ramuz's novels sentences abound which could be shortened and lightened without harming their denotative value, and a single example will suffice to illustrate an omnipresent tendency. In *La Grande Peur dans la montagne* this paragraph of only one sentence reveals just such an accumulation of detours and deviations:

One month, two months, went by; the Chairman continued to approach prudently with regard to his plan, the people that chanced to come his way, some shook their heads, but most had few objections; it was clear these old stories of twenty years ago were already indeed well and truly forgotten; and finally, the Chairman had only a small calculation to make; this one for and this one for, and that one against, which gave him a total on the one hand and another as well, two totals without much effort, first in his head, and then on paper; so he called together the Council.[15]

The thought expressed above meanders slowly, with stolid pedestrian logic, from an original project through actions, observations, reflections, and evaluations, before terminating in a decision. Both by the syntax and by the punctuation the author communicates admirably the sinuosities of an unsophisticated mental gait.

Elsewhere the slowness of the language becomes an imitative form which seeks to reproduce the quality of the physical movement of the character in question and, thereby, the uniform deliberateness of country life. And here one should insist on the creative talent of Ramuz in fashioning a style wholly suited to reflect the countryman's nature, but which is in no way a reproduction of any cantonal language. For the particular rhythm of a Ramuzian sentence is his own artistic and physical representation of time; and time for the poet, just as for the peasant, is essentially slow. In *Derborence* the inhabitants of Anzeindaz are described as they watch the changing sky on the night of the catastrophe:

but soon they were surprised to see the moon growing slightly darker, has faded, has become sad like when there is an eclipse, whilst the glow of the lantern became brighter, in contrast, making a circle of the short grass beneath their feet.
And it was then that they had seen this great pale cloud rise up before them. The silence gradually returned, the cloud grew ever longer behind the ridge which still hid the depths of Derborence, being there like a wall which climbed above a wall. It was like a fog, but it was slower, more weighty; and the mass of these vapors reached upwards, like dough rising, like when the baker has put the dough in his kneading-trough, and it swells in the trough, and it overflows from the trough.

mais ils se sont bientôt étonnés de voir la lune qui noircissait légèrement, qui s'est flétrie, qui est devenue triste comme quand il y a une éclipse, pendant que la lueur de la lanterne devenait plus nette, au contraire, faisant un rond sur l'herbe courte devant leurs pieds.
Et c'est alors qu'ils avaient vu cette grande nuée pâle se lever en avant d'eux. Le silence peu à peu revenait, elle, elle a grandi de plus en plus derrière la crête qui leur masquait encore les fonds de Derborence, étant là

comme un mur qui montait par-dessus un mur. C'était comme une grosse fumée, mais sans volutes, plate; c'était comme un brouillard, mais c'était plus lent, plus pesant; et la masse de ces vapeurs tendait vers en haut d'elle-même, comme de la pâte qui lève, comme quand le boulanger a mis la pâte dans son pétrin, et elle gonfle dans le pétrin, et elle dèborde du pétrin.[16]

The repetitions, the comparisons, the variations, and the abundance of relative clauses transpose not only the quality of the movement of "cette grande nuée pâle", but also the halting cerebral effort of the narrating peasant mind. Often this effect of diminished progress is even more apparent; this is the case, for example, towards the end of *Farinet* when the slow advance of the cortège bringing back the body of the hero is punctuated by the insistent tolling of the funeral bell.

The circumspection of the peasant is again translated most happily in the episode of *La Grande Peur dans la montagne* where Joseph is climbing towards the Fenêtre du Chamois. This passage also attests by an uneven and discontinuous form the labored steps and strenuous exertion of the protagonist:

Joseph walked with greater difficulty, more slowly, sinking in up to the knee. On his right hand and level with him, in the very continuation of the icy corridor he was crossing, a first crevasse, gaping, and that could be plumbed with the eye, because of its angle, marked the fracture point of the glacier.

Joseph marcha plus difficilement, plus lentement, enfonçant jusqu'au genou. A main droite et à sa hauteur, dans le prolongement même du névé qu'il traversait, une première crevasse largement ouverte et qu'on pouvait sonder de l'oeil, à cause de son inclinaison, marquait le point de rupture du glacier.[17]

These mimetic groupings, whether they result chiefly from a primitive peasant mentality or whether they approximate a physical movement, constitute a device of great importance in the process of narrative deceleration.

Elsewhere the frequent usage of simile fulfills a similar function of deceleration. Curiously, the figurative language of Ramuz is an area which has yet to inspire a detailed study.[18] Extended research in this field would undoubtedly confirm that the analogies, while numerous and original, derive from a very restricted universe and form for the most part a closed circle. Ramuz consistently describes peasant life and associated natural phenomena by comparing them with other elements from the same milieu. Inevitably this network of homogeneous imagery effaces the logical or social barriers that supposedly separate beings, animals, and objects and substitutes a world governed by *l'Analogie universelle*. However, if in fact this figurative language sought only to communicate the notion of harmonious unity, one would expect a marked predilection for metaphor, since metaphor insists far more forcefully than simile upon the idea of total identity. Yet, it is, on the contrary, simile which predominates in the novels of Ramuz where metaphor is relatively rare. Doubtless this preference for the substantial autonomy of the simile could weaken the concentrated coherence of the Ramuzian universe; but, as we shall see, it does result in notable advantages with respect to the temporal quality of the narrative. In contrast to the contracted brevity of metaphor, simile, because of an independent existence heralded by "comme," signals a pause, a delay, in the purely logical development of the story.

In *Farinet* for example a succession of juxtaposed similes, by rendering the style more "poetic," retards noticeably the unfolding of the story:

The brown and black cows were scattered points which he had to fix for a moment with his eyes before seeing them move, *large like ladybirds*, whilst at the corner of the roof the smoke was stiffly upright *like the feather of a jay*. The rocks around him were gleaming in the setting sun *like angels' wings*. He was at a height of almost three thousand meters, that is where every type of grass stops and only a few mosses can still be seen *like a little paint* on the flat of the rock. He was suspended in the air *like on a flying machine*. [19]

This device, a recurrent one in Ramuz, accumulates in the above paragraph five comparisons. The momentary abandonment of novelistic progression seems to invite the reader to mark time and to delay the logical advance of his own reading—a reading which having to follow a deliberately elongated figurative style will necessarily be slow.

V *Immobilization*

It would be foolish to deny that the necessity of some novelistic tissue, some evolving storyline, in any long work of literature makes the term "immobilization" indicative of a direction rather than of an actual goal. However, it is possible to discern in Ramuz's writings certain devices which, rather than fragmenting or decelerating the plot, succeed temporarily in arresting its unfolding and contribute forcefully to an impression of narrative stasis.

If, as I have earlier proposed, it is the state of Man, rather than the evolution of men, which is his fundamental principle, it is this which will necessarily determine much of the form we are at present surveying. In this respect there is a revealing sentence noted by Ramuz in his *Carnet*: "The notion of becoming is a straight line, the notion of being is a circle."[20]

This statement of Spinoza seems to suggest that the concept of "being" as different from "becoming" might find aesthetic expression in circular rather than linear construction. In purely novelistic terms such a distinction proposes a narrative which, instead of developing always away from the point of departure, in fact returns to it.

Among the works of the Swiss author, it is *Derborence* which reveals the most nearly perfect example of this, especially if one considers that the introductory allusion to the landslide in the first chapter is exergual. In that case the final chapter returns almost textually to the beginning of the second chapter:

"Derborence, the word sings sadly and softly in the head."[21]
"Derborence, the word sings softly; it sings to you softly and a little sadly in the head."[22]

These two passages and their continuations in the present tense, frame the rest of the story and, extending it beyond the merely incidental, confer an aura of eternity. For Spitzer, in his article "Le style de Ch.-F. Ramuz: le Raccourci Mystique," the existence of such a construction emphasizes the mystical heart he discerns in this particular novel: "The circular style is characteristic of the mystical event which starts and finishes nowhere."[23] But, for our purpose, the interest of such a structure resides primarily in its anti-narrative function, in its potential capacity to evoke a *poetic* state.

This same construction which determined the overall shape of *Derborence* can be traced in more modest guise than that of an entire novel. The first chapter of the second part of *Derborence*, situated exactly in the middle of the book in a structurally significant position, reveals a similar, if more limited circularity. On this occasion the final narrative return to the description of Antoine's disappearance, that same moment with which the chapter had commenced some five pages earlier, underlines the absence of temporal progression within the substance of the chapter. At the beginning we read "his head came out" and we rediscover that very action in the last paragraph: "Then too, his head came out, but it could not be seen because of the rocks which jutted out around it, hiding it completely."[24]

Between these two references the reader learns of the need to establish officially the exact size of the rockfall and to ensure the future solidity of the glacier—details which are completely inconsequential. The allusion to old Plan who continues to wander over the ill-fated slopes is scarcely more significant and adds little to the story line.

Yet more limited from a quantitative point of view, but equally revealing, is the following passage taken from *La Grande Peur dans la montagne:*

Barthélemy, on that morning, was coming and going with his wheelbarrow; Clou, he was a little below the chalet, with his tool. It was a place where the water which came down from the rockface tended to gather, spoiling the roots of the grass, so it was necessary to make a channel which let it run down below where it was needed. There are in this way a large number of these little jobs of all sorts in the mountains; there are more than enough to occupy you all day long, if one wants to take the trouble to do them properly, but Clou for the moment wasn't doing anything. As an outcrop prevented him from being seen, he had sat down, smoking his pipe, and was examining minutely the rocks in front of him, running his eye up and down from one end to the other, because of the hiding places that there were certainly there, but first one has to know where they are most likely to be found; whilst Barthélemy then was coming and going in front of the chalet.[25]

Here the narrator is describing the first workday at the summer pasture. The majority of the passage, contained between two references to Barthélemy's comings and goings, is endowed with multiple value: it evokes the eternal and repetitive aspect of this situation and it creates a certain suspense by imposing a period of waiting. But of far more importance for our study is the fact that by "looping the narrative loop" the story must recommence a second time at the same point as twenty-four lines earlier. The paragraph constitutes a pause.

Another device which endorses the consistency shown by Ramuz

in pursuit of his principal narrative aim is that by which the fictional
simultaneity of distinct sections of the text is emphasized. Let us
begin by considering the relatively banal case where a first event is
in the process of occurring and "pendant ce temps"—the classic
expression to link such episodes—in a different locality a second
event is taking place. Obviously the significance of these instances is
very restricted; for any author who wishes to depict two contemporaneous events must proceed in like manner, since the book,
even the line which reads from left to right, is consecutive in form.
But it is by comparison with this stereotyped beginning that will be
seen the value of the techniques of greater refinement conceived by
Ramuz to communicate simultaneity. In his first novel, Ramuz
treats in consecutive chapters Aline's day and Julien's day; only the
place changes, the temporal span remains identical. Similarly, in *La
Guerre dans le Haut-Pays* the simultaneous ascents of Félicie and
David, who are only separated by a peak towards which they are
striving, are described one after the other in the text, but with an
appropriate and conventional vocabulary to confirm the contem-
poraneity.

It is in *La Grande Peur dans la montagne* that there is to be found
the transition from a traditional technique to a more original and
modern version. Between the ninth and tenth chapters of this novel
the link is once again effected by the expression "Pendant ce
temps," the consecrated formula to which we have referred. However, this form, doubtless too "literary" and codified in Ramuz's
eyes, becomes increasingly replaced by simple juxtaposition which
fuses more completely the two occurrences. More and more, events
separated in actual space will be seen to be bound together without
distinction and without intellectualization in the consciousness of
the narrator. The psychological authenticity which accrues from a
practice that rejects accepted stylistic formalization is without doubt
the most remarkable result; but at the same time, juxtaposition
accentuates materially the temporal identity. In *La Grande Peur
dans la montagne*, at the very moment when Clou and the Président
are discussing the pasturage, Victorine and Joseph are climbing to
their favorite spot above the church:

Puis elle lui [Victorine à Joseph] souriait avec toutes ses dents qui faisaient
une barre blanche au bas de sa figure brune . . .
Ce sera comme vous voudrez, disait Clou . . . Moi, j'ai le temps, décidez-
vous, vous me direz . . .

Ills avaient le coucher de soleil derrière eux, derrière eux ils avaient la haie, ils s'asseyaient dans l'herbe.

Ils étaient bien, ayant le coucher de soleil et aussi la haie derrière eux. En avant d'eux, étaient les prés en pente au bas desquels il semblait que le village s'était laissé glisser, comme les gamins font sur leur fond de culotte.

On voyait que les toits se tenaient ensemble, s'étant mis ensemble, aimant à être ensemble, se serrant les uns contre les autres avec amitié;—et Clou disait que ça ne pressait pas;—on voyait aussi, derrière leurs barrières, les jardins, qui commençaient à *être verts et* à se tacher de jaune, de bleu, de rouge.

Then she [Victorine] smiled at him [Joseph] with her teeth making a white line at the bottom of her brown face . . .
"Just as you like," Clou was saying . . . "Me, I have the time, you decide and tell me . . ."
They had the sunset behind them, behind them they had the hedge, they were sitting in the grass.
They were fine, having the sunset and also the hedge behind them.
In front of them, were the sloping meadows to the foot of which it seemed that the village had let itself slip, like children do on the seat of their pants.

. . .

One could see that the roofs were clustered together having come together, happy to be together, grasping each other in friendship;—and Clou was saying that there was no hurry; one could also see, behind their gates, the gardens, which were beginning to be green and to take on patches of yellow, of blue, of red.[26]

This extract contains a succession of abrupt switches between two places which are so closely intertwined in the mind of the narrator that they even appear once, in the final paragraph, next to each other in the same sentence. This oscillating continues throughout the chapter and indeed even the following chapter, where once again the description of an ascent by Victorine and Joseph alternates with a conversation between the Président and a second charac-ter—this time Crittin.

This concentrated simultaneity which is to be found in many of Ramuz's works should not be confused with another related technique which seems to be derived more from the plastic arts than from literature. Critics have invoked the cubist painters with regard to Ramuz; and, certainly, one could plausibly associate their wish to present all the facets of a subject with Ramuz's device whereby an experience is related from two or more distinct points of view—"la vision stéréoscopique" as the theorists term it.[27] Whereas the examples of simultaneity that we have previously investigated revealed only temporal identity, stereoscopic vision means identity of time and space, only the narrator changes. Between the different accounts the story line shows no development; it is merely refiltered and redeployed. For example, in the third chapter of *Derborence*, precisely the same incident—the fateful avalanche—is passed through three separate collective consciousnesses: first "ceux d'Anzeindaz," then "ceux de Sanetsch," and, finally, "ceux de Zamperon."

In *La Grande Peur dans la montagne* the feverish descent of Joseph at the time of the unexpected appearance of Clou, and the first shots fired by the former, are recounted not only from the panic-stricken point of view of Joseph (a) but also as these actions are observed by Barthélemy (b) watching from below. Here are the relevant passages up to the first shot:

(a)

Joseph begins once more to climb down; but then the other was in front of him. He became large like a cloud.

He opens his arms.

"Ah! here you are . . . I knew it."

Joseph wanted to cry out, he feels his voice rasping in his throat.

"Go . . . go away! . . ."

Then: "Ah! you won't!" and his voice came back: he has just thought of his rifle; he stops, he pulls back the breech, he puts a cartridge in the gun.

Yet the other did not stop. He continued coming towards him.

And he only lifted his eyes again at the same time as he brought the rifle to his shoulder, but then he could see that the target was very close, having got enormously bigger: he only had time to fire.[28]

(b)

He [Barthélemy] has not understood the gesture that Joseph has suddenly made, when one of those gaps opened above him; but he then sees that Joseph is armed, he sees that gesture has been to bring his hand to his shoulder, then to take his rifle in his two hands; then the stony path could be seen to roll towards Joseph like water and it was as if someone was coming along the path, yet there was no one to be seen. There was nobody and at the same time there was a voice coming: then it was as if someone had begun to laugh. And Barthélemy: "What's he doing, becoming, it was whilst Joseph was running, then Joseph who was putting it to his shoulder, then the first shot crashes out.[29]

As I have already emphasized, the lesson brought back from

Ramuz's pilgrimage to Aix in 1917 was Cézanne's own conviction—
that the only true reality is the external world filtered through a
temperament, that nothing exists except in relation to an observer.
Passages such as those we have considered above confirm that belief
by their rejection of the restrictive artificiality of a constant and
omniscient narrative viewpoint. However, it is of more than marginal importance that to express a second time the same set of circumstances is to refuse any notable progression in the logical development of the plot.

It will have been observed that common to many of the above
examples is the element of repetition, and in itself simple use of
repetition merits an increasingly considerable place in the Swiss
author's mature narrative technique. Ramuz repeats and repeats
again words and phrases, reiterates exactly the sense of a sentence
in a subsequent sentence, and by this manipulation continues to
forge an atmosphere that is more emotive than rational, more poetic
than novelistic. Looking back in *René Auberjonois,* having
suggested that in every work of art there needs to be a balance
between the intellectual and the affective, Ramuz declares that it is
repetition—here in the form of the pleonasm—which communicates
the affective:

Let us take the example of the pleonasm. Reason does not allow the
pleonasm. A full stop having been indicated, reason is satisfied; for reason,
it is enough to grasp clearly; having once grasped, it proceeds at an even
pace, which makes it resent everything which might restrain it. Emotion, in
very contrary fashion, insists because of its determination to communicate
itself in its full intensity; it comes back to what it has already said, with other
words or the same, it repeats ("ressasse") willingly.[30]

Prenons l'exemple du pléonasme. La raison n'admet pas le pléonasme. Un
point ayant été indiqué, la raison est satisfaite; il lui suffit de saisir claire-
ment; une fois qu'elle a saisi, elle va plus loin et d'une allure égale, qui fait
qu'elle s'irrite de tout ce qui pourrait la retenir. L'émotion, bien au contraire, insiste à cause du souci qu'elle a de se communiquer dans toute son
intensité; elle revient à ce qu'elle a déjà dit, avec d'autres mots ou les
mêmes, elle ressasse volontiers.

The force of the original French word "ressasse" translates the
importance of a device which for Ramuz signals "emotion" and
which appears frequently in his writings to indicate the personal
involvement of the narrator. At one point in *Derborence,* when the

avalanche is being recounted as experienced by the inhabitants of Zamperon, the key passage contains several expressions which are repeated—"as if," "at the same time," "ground," "noise," "nor":

> The cheese buckets could be heard crashing down, the benches could be heard falling to the ground, the doors were shaken as if by two hands. At the same time there is movement and a rumbling; at the same time there is a crackling, at the same time a whistling; it was in the air, on the surface of the ground and under the ground, in a confusion of all the elements where one could no longer distinguish what was noise from what was movement, nor what these noises meant, nor whence they were coming, nor where they were going, as if it had been the end of the world.[31]

The fear and the incomprehension of these people is characterized most convincingly by the restricted and iterative vocabulary of their equally distraught "porte-parole". But *emotion* for Ramuz means *poetry*, and the insistent incantatory effect produced by such an accumulation evokes the hesitant circling of the melopea rather than the firm advance of the novel.

In considering Ramuz's particular use of repetition it is perhaps helpful to distinguish between those instances where iteration is purely thematic—merely conserving the sense—and those where it is formal—the expressions used being identical. Particularly effective amongst examples of the former because of their succinctness and also their immediate proximity to each other are the sentences in *La Grande Peur dans la montagne* which reveal Victorine walking towards the escarpment:

> She had arrived at the edge of the river, she began to walk upstream. The movement of the water was towards her; the water was coming ceaselessly against her, in little waves, then continuing its course.[32]

Precisely the same moment, when Victorine follows the river upstream, is expressed three times, but in three different ways; the opposition of nature, still largely passive at this point, is accentuated by the arrested narrative.

Formal repetition would seem to be the most striking instance of immobilization, for it is not unlike the poetic refrain. To reiterate the same thing, word for word, is to remain logically in the same position. Typographically, a remarkable example is the word AVIS which appears four times in capital letters towards the end of

Farinet, imposing on the reader successive returns to this official document. In similar fashion the temporal allusion, the twenty-second of June, punctuates the first part of *Derborence,* insisting repeatedly on a date which tolls with the heaviness of a death knell. Such repetition is capable of petrifying an event by attributing to it an abnormal intensity of meaning; for the reader is obliged to stay at, or return to, the point on which is fixed the eye of the narrator.

There is, for example, the moment in *Derborence* when Antoine reappears after having been buried alive for two months by the avalanche:

He puts out his head
[. . .] the head moved.
[. . .] this head appeared [. . .].
[. . .] when he puts out his head [. . .]
[. . .] only his head showed.
A poor wretch who emerges [. . .].
[. . .] a poor wretch who appears [. . .].
[. . .] he puts out his head.[33]

Il sort la tête
[. . .] la tête a bougé.
[. . .] cette tête s'est montrée [. . .].
[. . .] quand il sort la tête [. . .].
[. . .] sa tête a été seule à dépasser.
Un pauvre homme pourtant qui sort [. . .].
[. . .] un pauvre homme qui est apparu [. . .].
[. . .] il sort la tête.

This miraculous instant of resurrection, a fraction of a second in actual time, requires three full pages of text; and it is only later that this man, so long entombed, actually "raises his head." To linger thus on a moment of almost mystical significance necessitates the provisional renunciation of any advance in the story.

Since the very origins of literature, one of the fundamental problems that has confronted the writer is the irreducibly temporal nature of language: how to evoke the complexity and immediacy of an instantaneous sensation with a vehicle which refuses to stand still. In this quest, repetition, in its various guises, does afford a possible means of restraining the narrative and of halting, temporarily, the habitual progression of the reader.

Finally, since literature, at least as opposed to painting, is basically a continuum, inevitably the role of the verb is a major one; and this examination of the depth of Ramuz's antipathy towards traditional plot development would not be complete without reference to his efforts to avoid the spatio-temporal displacement inherent in verbal expression.

The present participle, for example, is able to express an action, a state, or a quality but seems to project only a limited movement in contrast to the autonomous force of a pure verbal tense. For the present participle has no absolute temporal value; it adjusts automatically to the tense of the clause to which it is attached and indicates at the very most an action dependent on the verb which it accompanies. Therefore, when a writer has frequent recourse to this particular form, there results a dilution of the active in comparison to that which might have been achieved by other, stronger, verbal expressions. Already in Flaubert the present participle is often evident, although according to Thibaudet this is largely because the refined sensibility of that author could not tolerate the dissonance of "qui" and "que."[34] In Ramuz there would seem to be an even greater predilection for the participial form:

From this side of the village, the fronts of the houses are in two colors, white at the bottom, brown at the top; from the other, their lower, back part hardly tops the narrow passage which opens up between them and another row of buildings; being thus black and white at the front, being at the front tidy and well-kept, like hives in a garden; at the back, very dark, all over the place, and then casting a shadow on the always muddy passage.

De ce côté-ci du village, les maisons ont des façades de deux couleurs, blanches dans le bas, brunes dans le haut; de l'autre, leur derrière plus bas domine à peine l'étroit passage qui s'ouvre entre elles et une autre rangée de constructions; étant ainsi noires et blanches par devant, étant par devant bien disposées et arrangées, comme des ruches dans un jardin; par derrière toutes noires, mises là pêle-mêle, et puis faisant de l'ombre sur le passage toujours boueux.[35]

In this extract taken from *Derborence* the three present participles, "étant," étant," and "faisant," insist on the state of the houses and establish certain characteristics—reinforcing in the second half of the paragraph the tense of the main clause.

Elsewhere, a grammatical disjunction may separate the participle from the clause on which it is supposedly dependent. This is the case, for example, in the following passage taken from *Farinet:*

It's fine here, said the master . . . From here, he said, you can see everything and you can see everywhere. In front and at the back, to the right and
to the left, downwards and upwards . . .
Making a circle with his arm, tilting back his head, then bringing it forward.
And it was true. But Farinet, having taken hold of the telescope, had
immediately turned falsely to the rocks.

Là on est bien, a dit le maître . . . De là a-t-il dit, on voit tout, et on voit
partout. Devant et derrière, à droite et à gauche, en bas et en haut . . .
Faisant aller son bras en rond autour de lui, renversant la tête, puis la
ramenant en avant. Et c'était vrai. Mais Farinet, ayant empoigné la lon-
gue-vue, s'était tout de suit tourné trompeusement vers les rochers.[36]

and also in another passage where Josephine brings food to Farinet,
and where the verb indicating direct speech is omitted:

"Well! I haven't eaten a thing since ten o'clock this morning. You realise,
that's quite a time."
Being full of good humour and appetite, slicing into the loaf, stabbing with
the point of his knife the slices of dried meat:
"Three weeks or more, that's a lot!"

Eh bien! je n'ai rien mangé depuis dix heures, ce matin. Tu vois, ça fait un
bout de temps.
Etant plein de bonne humeur et d'appétit, taillant dans la miche, piquant
avec la pointe de son couteau les tranches de viande sèche:
Trois semaines et plus, ça compe![37]

Communicating a physical autonomy which supersedes the spoken, and faithful to the uncultured linguistic awkwardness of the
peasant, these present participles refer without explicit attachment
to what has preceded. Like misplaced stage directions, they logically accompany the words which they follow and constitute, therefore, a halt and a latent narrative return to a separate grammatical
element.

A parallel reduction of verbal force has been noted by C.R. Parsons,[38] who points to the relatively high frequency in Ramuz's
writings of certain verbs which express a state rather than an action.
This wealth, chiefly of existential verbs like "être," "y avoir," "se
trouver," is undoubtedly a major factor in the question of narrative
stasis we are examining. When Ramuz repeatedly chooses to replace
the verb "aller"—which signals action par excellence—by "être," he
is underlining unequivocally his own narrative direction. When he

chooses to write in *Derborence*, "Thérèse avait été se coucher," rather than, "Thérèse était allée se coucher," it is at least in part because he is more concerned with the state than the action. The state of being stretched out in bed facilitates for Thérèse the important *rêverie* concerning Antoine which follows—the act of going to bed is of no significance.

Again, at the moment when Thérèse abandons her husband, "être" replaces "aller" with very real overtones:

He [Antoine] was sleeping, his arms crossed, his mouth slightly open. And from his mouth there came at regular intervals a loud even noise like that of a wood rasp; so that, in her distress, Thérèse had not had the courage to sleep at his side, as was her duty as a wife.
She had been to spend the night at her mother's house.

Il [Antoine] dormait, les bras en croix, la bouche entr'ouverte. Et de sa bouche sortait à intervalles bien égaux un bruit fort et marqué comme celui d'une lime à bois: de sorte que, dans son malaise, Thérèse n'avait pas eu le courage de se coucher à son côté, comme c'était son devoir de femme.
Elle avait été passer la nuit chez sa mère.[39]

Because of the choice of "être" the last line in the above extract rightly emphasizes the time duration of that night, rather than Thérèse's journey to the other house as would have been the case if the expression had read, "Elle était allée passer"; for it is this night of sin against her duty as a wife which prepares the way for the redemption and apotheosis with which the novel concludes. By virtue of its existential value "être" focuses the attention on a fixed point and is therefore opposed to normal prose chronology.

The different forms of the paradigm "y avoir," a second existential expression, also appear with unusual frequency in Ramuz's writings. In the following passage where Justin and Nendaz are shown journeying towards Derborence, the entire scene is perceived integrally without any temporal subordination or anteriority:

But, at that hour, and as the moon had just gone in, one could only just distinguish the unevenness of its surface, which was considerable and quite awkward, for the two men had no lantern. There are round stones which slide away under the sole, there are bits of shale which slip, there are pebbles which jut out and on which the foot catches.

Mais, à cette heure, et comme la lune venait de se cacher, c'est tout juste si on distinguait les inégalités de sa surface qui étaient grandes, et assez gênantes, car les deux hommes n'avaient point de lanterne. Il y a des pierres rondes qui fuient sous la semelle, il y a des feuilles de schiste qui basculent, il y a des cailloux qui font saillie et où bute la pointe du pied.[40]

Three times the author insists in the second sentence on the details of these surface "inégalités." The choice of an expression—"il y a"—which invokes the presence, the condition, of these objects, as much as recourse to the present tense, arrests once again the narrative.

The ultimate point in this tendency towards verbal reduction, beyond static and existential forms, is the absence of any verb. Without a verb there is likely to be *no* action, *no* movement—and Ramuz was clearly conscious of this:

Finally, the verb is very often absent [from his writings]. The impression, the state alone remains, therefore immobility; the verb which marks action is indeed no longer necessary; it would even kill the vividness of the impression by making things somehow active.[41]

This search for "the impression" was not unaffected by Ramuz's closeness to the painters of his period. Numerous sentences, sometimes entire paragraphs, aspire by their a-verbal character to a quality of immobility that is closer to the pictorial than the literary. Thus, in *Derborence*, the reader is presented with something akin to a sketch as Antoine is relating his experience under the rockfall:

"We'd have to count; me, I can't. You count," he [Antoine] said to Nendaz. "How many is it?"
"That's seven weeks and even a bit more than seven weeks. It will be eight weeks."
"No, really!"
Seated at his table surrounded by people, a glass in front of him.

Il faudrait compter; moi, je ne peux pas. Comptez, vous, disait-il [Antoine] à Nendaz. Ça fait sept semaines et même un peu plus de sept semaines. Ça va faire huit semaines.
Pas vrai!
Assis à sa table entouré de monde, un verre devant lui.[42]

With deft strokes in the final paragraph of the above extract, the author captures a totally motionless scene, a still narrative frame.

VI   *The Universality of the Vision*

While I regret the alarming destructiveness of this provisional critical vivisection, I must now point to other co-present devices which serve to establish the universality of that, as yet undelimited, enduring quality which Ramuz descerns in Man.

As I have endeavored to point out at every opportunity during this study there can be few serious novelists of the twentieth century whose labors have languished so long in undeserved oblivion, particularly in America and Great Britain, as the one we are considering. Strangely, the most widespread criticism of his work is the one which under close textual examination is the most difficult to justify—that of regionalism. From the early condemnations of his "provincialismes barbares" to the present-day tendency to relegate him to a succinct footnote in a chapter on Giono, Ramuz has continued to suffer from the inexplicable blindness of most critics to the extraordinary coherence of a narrative technique in which a multitude of devices converge forcefully towards an impression of universality. Throughout a life devoted entirely to his art, Ramuz never ceased to affirm and present a vision of a world in which the actions and events of any period or situation are no more than the present incarnation of an eternal prototype.

VII   *Universal Person*

The curious transposition achieved by the art of those writers who wish above all to fashion a fiction which resembles reality supposes, necessarily, a complex relationship between "personnage" and "personne." Ducrot and Todorov, in their excellent *Dictionnaire encyclopédique des sciences du langage*, insist that a link between the two is obligatory despite the essentially linguistic nature of "personnage":

The problem of character ["personnage"] is primarily linguistic [. . .] it does not exist outside of words [. . .]. However, to refuse any relationship between character ["personnage"] and person ["personne"] would be absurd: the former *represent* persons, according to the modes of fiction.[43]

This link exists inevitably in Ramuz, but the individuality implied in the notion of person tends to disappear and is replaced by a constant emphasis on those qualities which are permanent in man, those which are opposed to the particular. Thus, paradoxically, the characters of a Ramuzian novel are characterized especially by their lack of characterization. We are already far from the predominant practice of the preceding century, when with slow fastidious method a writer sought to construct a convincing biography and psychology. Beyond person, it is *Person* that Ramuz attempts to translate— "Homme" rather than "hommes." This minute artifice of typography, taken from Ramuz himself, conveys the essence of his attitude towards his everyday heroes. Close scrutiny of the different texts of his maturity reveals that this fundamental Man referred to above is represented by Ramuz in three main ways: first, by the choice of characters who are truly exemplary; then, by the evocation of a narrator who embraces in a collective consciousness reader, writer, and fictional creations; finally, by the forging of a language of greater authenticity than conventional class-ridden French.

The quest for authenticity which typifies the content of any novel of Ramuz determines also the nature of his characters, for they are required in their turn to manifest an a-social purity rare in the still-stratified twentieth century. It is, therefore, the countryman who continually recurs as hero; it is in him that Ramuz discovers Being, stripped of the palimpsest trappings that individualize the bourgeois:

I only distinguish a being at the roots of the elementary. He only appears to me fully and, so to speak, in full action when he is still fresh from birth [. . .]. The more complex he becomes, the less contact there is with deep substance, one no longer gets past the bark.[44]

Rejecting the divisiveness of all social and cultural acquisition, Ramuz discovers in his own Switzerland, more precisely in the mountainous region of Le Valais and the lakeside Canton du Vaud, not the Swiss peasant but primordial man ("fresh from birth") whose origins return beyond pre-history. Renouncing vigorously the limitations of regionalism, Ramuz appropriates in his Valaisan and Vaudois novels characters of universal significance and emphasizes only the constants of humanity.

In 1936 Ramuz reiterates yet more fully—and most provocatively—the strength of his continuing predilection on the occasion of his receiving the Schiller award. In a speech which is tantamount to an artistic credo, Ramuz ignores those who derided him as a poor writer and dares to consider himself in relation to the most classical of French authors, in relation to Racine himself. Thus, the peasants who people Ramuz's novels are to be interpreted, because of their similar extra-social situation, as the current manifestation of the "rois de Racine":

Men tend to differ increasingly as their ideas become more complicated, in my desire to see them resemble each other, I used a radical ploy, eliminating the idea which divides and the interests which separate; I made . . .or at least I should have liked the peasant I envisaged to be, at the other end of hierarchy, quite symmetrical to Racine's kings who were only kings or were only chosen kings because they thus escaped all types of social convention which might have made them in some way prisoners of themselves; who are only kings in order to be better placed to yield freely to their human passions. Racine's kings are men divested of the accessory anecdotes of human life; the peasant, as I have conceived him, and due allowance being made, is a man of that same quality, a man somewhat outside the, let us say, bourgeois society of today, and therefore outside time.[45]

Clearly, Ramuz's peasant is intended to represent a human essence no longer subject to temporal flux. Indeed, even the characters in Ramuz's writings who would seem to suffer most from the inevitable contagion of a particular plot and are transparently tainted with personality, even they retain a considerable permanence. As if in reaction against the corrosive force of precise novelistic situation, Ramuz seems to "divest" many of his characters of their rare individual traits, seeks to depersonalize them still further. In other words, that human quintessence which exists for Ramuz at the core of each personality requires, at times, even for the peasant, to be laid bare by the final removal of all remaining distinctive accoutrements. In *La Grande Peur dans la montagne* the identity crisis suffered by Joseph largely on account of the dissolvent power of darkness presupposes a concomitant loss of individuality. The deliberate suppression of the person, in direct contrast to the maturation of a traditional *Bildungsroman* where the protagonist develops as the story unfolds, finally removes any element which belongs specifically to Joseph and renders exemplary the fatal events which follow:

He took a few steps and he was deep into the night. He had just entered the wood, he no longer knew if he even existed, so completely had his person

been suppressed, so that he had to feel for his body with his hand; he had to run his hand over the clothes covering his body over the rough cloth over the buttons, over the facings of the pockets, over the linen shirt.
So he was there a moment, and he existed for a moment, then there was again nothing more than the pure spirit of his thought, wondering: "Where am I? What am I doing?"[46]

In this passage the process of decharacterization passes through initial doubt and virtual loss of body substance to terminate in the final paragraph in a reduction to the "pure spirit" who poses the questions and whose anguish is soon to be shared by all.

Gilbert Guisan, in his book *C.–F. Ramuz ou le génie de la patience*, points to a convergent technique—the ellipsis of the subject, noun, or pronoun.[47] According to Guisan such a device is rather more artistic than rustic and figures primarily in the first editions of the early novels before being more or less abandoned by Ramuz in later versions.

Perhaps more meaningful and certainly more subtle are those similar techniques at the end of *Derborence* which also attempt to transpose to the level of paradigm that which would otherwise be conventional incident. The exergual quotation taken from the *Dictionnaire géographique*, with which the novel begins, may be considered to constitute an immediate generalization by its use of the imprecise "un pâtre." The return in the last pages of the novel to the same indefinite vocabulary reinforces the structural circularity by relegating to a minor position the accidental quality of those details which form the central body of the text. In these concluding pages one is no longer faced with a short isolated passage but with a complex and conscious progression in which first Thérèse, then Antoine, emerges from the historical and geographical context to become eminently symbolic. It is Plan, by addressing Thérèse on three consecutive occasions as "Femme" despite knowing her personally, who announces this evolution beyond superficial story line. Then, a few pages later, Antoine undergoes a similar process of depersonalization, indeed, in his case, of dehumanization, as he becomes first a "point" and then a "patch":

Because of the distance Antoine was already up there little more than a white point, the color of his trousers merging with the dark spots between the stones. Only the little white patch of his shirt, but happily it was changing position and always moving, the other colours on the stony ground being motionless in contrast.[48]

Stripped of his particular identity, Antoine is now ready to assume vaster proportions; and his full significance is revealed on the following page as the initial exergue is twice repeated with little reformulation:

It is the story of a shepherd who has been captured under the stones, and here he is returning to the stones as if he could no longer do without them.
It is the story of a shepherd who has disappeared for two months, and he has reappeared, but he disappears again.[49]

Antoine has now become the "pâtre" or "berger" of the *Dictionnaire géographique*; the Valaisan peasant is increasingly recognizable as eternal, elementary, Man. Subsequently, both characters, Antoine and Thérèse, come together again after the anguish of their long separation; and the miracle of the instant of union and harmony which crowns the book is not restricted to two individuals but opens onto the infinite:

It is a man with a woman.
The five who were there had in front of them the mountain with its ramparts and towers; and it is evil, it is all-powerful, but here a feeble woman has stood up aganst it and she has conquered it, because she loved, because she loved.
She will have found the words which had to be said, she will have come with her secret; having life inside her, she has been where there was no more life, she brings back that which is living from the middle of that which is dead.
"Hohé!"
They shout out through their hands the cry of the mountain; they hear their cry which comes back to them and it is that the reply has come from above.
A man's voice, a woman's voice. And it was her and it was him; now one could see that the man was helping the woman in the difficult sections; where the rockface was steep he jumped down first, he took her in his arms.[50]

By a neutral and depersonalized vocabulary Ramuz communicates once again the exemplariness which is the basis of each of his characters. Without names at this decisive moment, Antoine and Thérèse have become quite simply "a man" and "a woman," "she" and "him." In fact, invisible for a brief period, they are only present by virtue of their "voice" detached from any identifiable body. In the last paragraph of the above passage, having underlined the independent symbolic values of the two characters, Ramuz establishes definitively the fusion of this couple ("he took her in his arms") by an embrace of supreme proportions. Despite their identical extra-social position, in contrast to the Racinian hero who, finally, remains alone, Ramuz's peasants have come to incarnate a fraternity which knows no frontiers, the essential unity of all human beings.

It would seem then that through the choice and treatment of his characters Ramuz is able to generalize the experience he is relating and make it the experience of Man himself. In order to convey yet more fully this notion of collectivity Ramuz goes further and groups together in his novels narrator, peasant, and reader, associates them to himself and creates in his narrative a dimension which is ultimately ontological. In the best novels, which follow that fertile manifesto *Adieu à beaucoup de personnages*, the principle of collectivity, distantly related both to the unanimism of Jules Romains and the social lyricism of Whitman—two authors much admired by Ramuz—is always fundamental to the narrative style of the Swiss author.

In this respect the most obvious mark by which the author attests his empathy with the novelistic characters is his emotion. This affective presence of the narrator, extremely rare in traditional writing, continually emphasizes how much the fate of the peasants is shared. For example, from the very beginning of *La Grande Peur dans la montagne* the reader encounters expressions such as "le bon pays" and "heureusement que l'hiver avait été très froid" in the narrative itself. Explicit attitudes and affective appellations like these confirm the bucolic blood of the one who is telling the story. In *Derborence* those who come to quantify the fatal landslide are called by the narrator "messieurs de la ville," suggesting not only the contrasting rural provenance of the speaker but also a certain typical social awareness.

Undoubtedly one of the most predictable and enduring traits of the countryman, one by which he will always be recognized, is his intolerance of new methods. Thus, a fiercely conservative opinion, almost italicized by the parentheses which surround it, suffices to unveil the narrator of *Farinet*:

They [the bars] were however both strong, because they were forged on the anvil in the olden days [when they still knew what forging was]: nevertheless they were now severed at their tops and level with the stone, both of them . . . .[51]

However, it is above all at moments of extreme tension and anxiety that the narrator reveals a sensibility identical to those whose story he is recounting. Such is the justification, for instance, of the heartfelt "Alas!" which interrupts and colors the factual description of the procession accompanying Barthélemy's stretcher in *Derborence*:

There are arms which rise, hands are placed flat on either side of a head, the men on the other hand lower theirs the Chairman, Justin, Rebord, Nendaz, the others—very few and for a long time alas! very few because of all the deaths that there have been up there; it's a small village, a small village of goats, women, children, old men.[52]

In the above passage the narrator does not simply register and report the suffering of the villagers; he feels with them the tragedy of death, he is transparently of their company.

By parallel devices the collective experience related by these rural bards is amplified further, beyond the confines of country life, to include the reader himself. In his attempts to universalize the significance of the events described, and long before the Nouveau Roman, this maligned Swiss writer manipulated with great skill the entire pronominal range, profiting in particular from the unifying force of "on," "nous," and "vous."

While remaining widespread, the least frequent of these pronouns in Ramuz is the second-person plural, which is, significantly, the most modest in its grammatical application. "Vous" in a third-person narrative invites, or demands, the collaboration in the action of the addressee. A link is thus established between the protagonist(s) and the reader. In *La Grande Peur dans la montagne* this link becomes total identification as the reader seems to be substituted corporeally for Joseph:

Joseph marcha plus difficilement, plus lentement, enfonçant jusqu'au genou. A main droite et à sa hauteur, dans le prolongement même du névé qu'il traversait, une première crevasse largement ouverte et qu'on pouvait sonder de l'oeil, à cause de son inclinaison, marquait le point de rupture du glacier. Plus en arrière, celui-ci s'élevait en pente douce jusqu'à une sorte de col qui s'ouvrait sur le ciel, et c'est là qu'on a vu paraître enfin le soleil: un soleil comme vu à travers du papier huilé, qui a été vu, qui ne l'est plus;—qui paraît,qui a disparu. C'est qu'une arête noire était venue se mettre *entre lui et vous; entre lui et Joseph*, il y avait eu cette nouvelle barrière à la recontre de laquelle Joseph allait.

Joseph walked with greater difficulty, more slowly, sinking in up to his knee. On his right hand and level with him, in the very continuation of the icy corridor he was crossing, a first crevasse gaping open and that one could plumb with the eye, because of its slope, marked the fracture point of the glacier. Further back, the latter rose gently up towards a sort of pass which opened in the sky, and it was there that the sun at last appeared: a sun seen as if through grease-proof paper, which has been seen, which is no longer; which appears, which has disappeared. It is that a black ridge had come *between it and you; between it and Joseph;* there had been this new barrier towards which Joseph was going.[53]

The "vous" which anticipates "Joseph" in the last sentence of this passage, situated in exactly the same grammatical context, elucidates the preceding "on" (1.3) and plunges the reader into the same snowfield through which the protagonist is laboring. However, the presence of "on" in the above passage necessitates a remark concerning our interpretation of "vous", for "vous" is also, in popular language, the objective case of "on". Nevertheless, relative to "on", because of an evident association with the second person, "vous", and its derivatives, impose a striking fusion of reader and character, a fusion of which Ramuz was doubtless conscious. Indeed at times the author may even insist textually on this distinction. In the following passage the reader is included among those who relieve the post which is supposed to prevent any contact between the villagers and those above quarantined with the diseased animals—the "vous" of the last sentence being clearly distinct from the "on" which is the subject of the main verb:

Quatre hommes, six fois par jour, ça en faisait vingt-quatre par jour; or, à peine s'ils étaient une centaine d'hommes au village, de sorte que votre tour revenait deux fois par semaine à peu près et souvent au milieu de la nuit. Les tours étaient inscrits sur un papier. On venait à deux heures du matin vous appeler sous vos fenêtres.

Four men, six times a day, that made twenty-four a day; well, there were scarcely a hundred men in the village, so that your turn came up about twice a week and often in the middle of the night. The hours were written on paper. Someone came to call you at two in the morning outside your window.[54]

As opposed to the preceding example, the "vous" in the above passage proposes a rapprochement with sundry individuals in a group rather than with a single person.

A study of the first-person plural may well follow more or less the same schéma. But, as different from "vous," "nous" entails "je," that is to say that in a narrative this pronoun necessarily includes the narrator. Its use may again be restricted to a small group or even be enlarged to involve the entire village. In *La Grande Peur dans la montagne*, after the departure of Victorine at the end of the feast, the appearance of the first-person plural suggests a sudden fraternity, a sort of hustling together, in the face of a hostile silence of the narrator and those of the pasturage—and even, perhaps, of the reader:

Up above, a few crows were still wheeling around the rockface before returning to the crevices where they nest and have cried out again perhaps, but with cries not strong enough to reach here, and come to us; so there is only the noise of the water which does not count, and there has been only the great silence and the great void, where Joseph gets up because he was cold.[55]

Là-haut, quelques corneilles tournaient encore contre les parois avant de regagner les fissures du roc où elles nichent, et ont crié encore peut-être, mais avec des cris pas assez forts pour qu'ils puissent venir jusqu'ici, et venir à nous; alors il n'y a plus que le bruit de l'eau qui ne compte pas; il n'y a plus eu que le grand silence et que ce grand vide, où Joseph se lève parce qu'il avait froid.

More frequently, however, "nous" or its derived forms communicates a solidarity with all the villagers, a solidarity which is again most clearly evident at moments of great anxiety or suffering. During these periods the narrator seems to live even more intensely the story he is recounting, and the misfortunes of the characters become definitely his own:

As soon as a beast had been milked, it moved off. One after another, they have moved off like this, going to lie down somewhere in the pasturage for the night; there were now only two or three who were still there;—so it was possible to know the extent of our misfortune, the ground having cleared we began to know our misfortune here too, and our shame, whilst Barthélemy got up again, passing once more his arm over his brow, shaking before him his hand with fingers open.[56]

Sitôt qu'une bête avait été traite, elle s'écartait. L'une après l'autre, elles se sont ainsi écartées, allant se coucher quelque part dans le pâturage pour la nuit; il n'y en avait plus maintenant que deux ou trois qui étaient encore là;—alors on a pu connaître l'étendue de notre malheur, le terrain s'étant dégagé, on a commencé à connaître notre malheur, ici aussi, et notre honte, pendant que Barthélemy se relevait, passant de nouveau le bras sur son front, secouant devant lui sa main aux doigts ouverts.

The milk which Barthélemy spills uselessly on the ground is the symbol of a tragedy which far exceeds the particular circumstances of this event. Without seeking to establish a rule one could contend that the Ramuzian narrator, susceptible to the poignancy of certain moments of the action, is himself so affected at such times that he feels compelled to employ consistently the pronoun "nous" and the related possessive adjective. It must be admitted in passing that "notre" is often used in the spoken language as the possessive adjective for "on," a popular form which recalls the use of "vous" as the objective case of "on" to which we have already referred. Rather than recommending a series of rigid and indefensible divisions, I am merely attempting to sketch the pronominal tendencies of an author-linguist.

The final question to be posed in this inventory of Ramuz's pronouns is on the relative position of "on." Without intending to treat any particular writer, M. Cressot establishes in his book *Le Style et ses techniques* a hierarchy which is admirably suited to Ramuz: "It seems that 'nous' expresses a greater solidarity; with 'on' the idea of solidarity is more of the mind, the persons involved less clearly designated."[57]

Thus, "on" would possess a plural value like "nous," but would also suggest a somewhat indeterminate quality, a collectivity in which the constituent elements are not clearly defined. Nevertheless, Cressot does insist that the reader and the writer, at least, are likely to figure amongst those invoked by this pronoun: "In a narrative, 'on' instead of 'ils' allows the writer to associate himself and to associate the reader with the action."[58]

The use of "on" is so widespread in Ramuz's novels that nearly every page could offer a representative example. It is merely worth emphasizing that the recurrent use of "on" would seem to allow a further amplification, beyond "vous" and "nous," resituating the singularity of the plot in the widest possible context. If "vous" invokes the presence of the reader and "nous" that of the narrator—perhaps at times of the reader, "on" is the final point in the development towards universality. The critical act never recaptures the creative, and it would be naïve to claim that this pronominal grid I have proposed is that of the author; however, my analysis does bring out in yet another sphere the fundamental tendency of the Ramuzian aesthetic—a global intuition which seeks to weld into a single Person, author, reader, and character.

Despite the denigration to which I have made allusion, Ramuz therefore should rather be considered as occupying an honorable position among those who have endeavored to render language more subtle and expressive. If one considers that Mallarmé advocated the disintegration of rational grammar and that Flaubert revolutionized sundry aspects of traditional literary formulation, Ramuz may well be seen as the writer who finally liberated the language of the novel and detached it from any particular social class.

This new freedom reveals itself equally in the remarkable similarity between the language of the dialogue and the language of the narrative, for the former overflows into the latter. The consistent linguistic tone which results indicates a notable reduction in distance between the voice of the narrator and that of the characters; and, once more, the narrator is added to this essential grouping that the peasants represent. For this reason, Ramuz's language, neither Parisian nor Vaudois, neither archaic nor ultra-modern, but deliberately omnispatial and omnitemporal, merits a closer analysis.

The origin of his distinct new mode of expression is primarily the spoken language, notably that used by the Swiss countryfolk with whom Ramuz was acquainted. But, as I have already contended, this should only be seen as a partial origin, for the language which appears in Ramuz's novels does not belong to any specific community which has ever existed in reality.

The most obvious anti-literary element is the banishment of the past historic as the normal narrative tense. Already in *La Grande Peur dans la montagne* the instances of this tense (236 examples) are substantially less than those of the perfect (855) and the present (1166), and this tendency becomes even clearer with the publication a few years later of *Derborence* in which there are to be found only fourteen cases of the past historic. *Farinet* (31 examples), published between *La Grand Peur dans la montagne* and *Derborence*, reveals an intermediate stage in the same gradual diminishing of numbers. The abandonment of this tense, already prohibited in the spoken language, is not surprising, for its use by a character-narrator describing almost orally the events would smack of either the pedant or the provincial—and Ramuz wanted neither. Moreover, and of greater significance for our argument, in literature the past historic—"ce temps factice",[59] "indice de la fiction"[60]—betokens *creation;* its presence would therefore damage the authenticity of the language and tend to repulse the reader rather than to embrace him.

However, it is largely the predominance of a neutral vocabulary in his narrative which confirms a proximity to speech. Apart from rare exceptions there is never a word or a phrase which does not belong to the lexical material of Gougenheim's Standard French. The source of reference utilized for the latter's *L'Elaboration du Français Fondamental* was likewise the spoken language and it is therefore not unexpected that Gougenheim should point out in his lists, as do I for Ramuz, the high frequency of "ça," "on," "beau," "joli," "petit," "aller," "dire," "être," "avoir," etc.[61] The classical quest for elegant variants in literary language is replaced in Ramuz, as in the spoken language, by the untiring repetition of the same simple word.

It is again this auto-limitation which engenders in the narrative style of the Swiss author certain unusual grammatical forms. For example, the use of a preposition in terminal position permits the reiteration of the same verb ("venir contre" instead of "s'approcher," "venir en-bas" instead of "tomber"). Within the narrative too there is a predilection for expressions which are clearly conversational in tone. Familiar appellations such as "la grosse Apolline" and "le vieux Munier" are disseminated through all the novels and accentuate not only the affinity between narrator and character to which we have already referred, but also the non-rhetorical nature of the style. The addition of superfluous words like "et alors" and "et plus" is typical of casual oral delivery and contributes to the impression of everyday banality. At all times the simplicity of the sentence structure, where juxtaposition and coordination are preferred to any complex subordination, emphasizes the naïve, primary, quality of the language.

"Langue régionaliste" exclaimed many critics—but in reality the number of "Romand" expressions is extremely limited. D. Haggis, for example, can only find *four* regionalist words in *Aimé Pache peintre vaudois,* a novel of some three hundred pages and certainly there is no increase in the novels of maturity.[62] The use of regionalisms would be too restrictive and superficial a technique to communicate even the peasant let alone Man. The language in the novels is rather, resolutely, that of the unlettered, a language which seeks to be authentic, a language to be used by a humanity devoid of social stratification. Common to both narrator and character and so close to the "français fondamental" of the ideal reader, this language is yet another level on which Ramuz strives to weld together all those who participate in the creative act. By such devices he projects his villages beyond the particular and accedes at last in novels like *La Grande Peur dans la montagne, Farinet,* and *Derborence* to that notion of "Personne" to which he had aspired already in *Adieu à beaucoup de personnages:*

Me participating in them, them merged into me, me merged into them; me remaining in that *Person* whence after all I came.[63]

VIII   *Universal Time*

The representation of time has become during the twentieth century an important point of contact between the different art forms as well as constituting a major aspect of literature. In Ramuz the desire to evoke a collectivity rather than an individual finds a temporal parallel in a series of attempts to replace consecrated linear time:

While there is no longer past, nor future—there is only around us one great immobility of time, as when one looks at a vast peaceful landscape.[64]

The desire to amalgamate past and future into "one great immobility of time," into an eternal present, is rationalized most clearly in the beautiful pages of *René Auberjonois,* where this time Ramuz insists on the notion of "a perfect continuity."

The past and the present rejoined, the life of men, the life of things, nothing archaeological nothing to do with a museum, everything which has served still serves and will doubtless still serve: there is no opposition, it is a perfect continuity.[65]

It is interesting to observe that it is from a book written on a *painter* that we have extracted one of the best definitions which could be conceived for the creative art of Ramuz himself. If one were so unfashionable as to accept the fundamental distinction enunciated by Lessing in his *Laokoön* between literature as an art of time and painting as an art of space, then Ramuz, by his preference for the static rather than the changing, may well be justified in his repeated claim that his true vocation was pictorial art.

Nevertheless, far from being an incompetent grammarian, Ramuz manifests a thorough awareness of the rich nuances of language, particularly with respect to the potential values of the different tenses; in addition, far from being a writer without talent, Ramuz cointrived to weave into the fabric of his novels several elements which dilate the story towards the infinite. In this respect the two aspects of time which will preoccupy us are the neutralized temporality resulting from a skillful handling of tense and the expanded temporality engendered by expressions and allusions of a historical nature.

Without returning to the question of factitiousness, the renunciation of the past historic to which I have already alluded by an author seeking to eternalize the significance of his work was inevitable, for this tense is directly opposed to Ramuz's own orientation. The past historic, bound by the idea of completed event, expressing conventionally a series of past actions, not only detaches from the present but even tends to condense the expanse of time (il vécut cinquante ans"). Clearly, the fine precision of this tense is far removed from the universality intended by Ramuz.

In order to communicate a more or less similar temporality as the past historic, Ramuz profits from the greater elasticity of the perfect tense. The link with the present evoked by the very structure of this past tense was far more appropriate to a writer who saw time as unbroken. The other past tense which abounds in Ramuzian narrative is the imperfect, capable, even more than the perfect, of translating the notion of *state*. The imperfect by dwelling on an act or event may transform it into a tableau and, further, in many contexts occupies a position astride past and present.

While acknowledging cursorily the importance of these two tenses in Ramuz's novels, one must point out as far more revealing their progressive reduction in successive works, even within the mature period of Ramuz's writing. In this respect the figures encountered in an examination of *La Grande Peur dans la montagne*,

Farinet, and *Derborence* are symptomatic of the general trend. The perfect tense—855 in *La Grande Peur dans la montagne*—is notably diminished in subsequent novels—566 in *Farinet* and 561 in *Derborence*—but less, proportionally, than the imperfect—2081 in *La Grande Peur dans la montagne,* 1438 in *Farinet,* and 1199 in *Derborence.* Even if one takes into account very slight variations in length between these novels, this reduction of tenses which seemed to correspond admirably to the author's conception of time remains surprising. The explanation becomes apparent in complementary figures to those just quoted, for there is an equivalent increase in instances of the present tense—1166 in *La Grande Peur dans la montagne,* 1211 in *Farinet,* and 1999 in *Derborence.* Clearly, it is this tense which must be acknowledged as the key to the Swiss author's primary temporality.

The predominance in Ramuz's novels of the perfect, the imperfect, and, above all, the present tenses is further elucidated by reference to the theoretical statements of Ducrot and Todorov on the relationship of the different tenses with the present of the narrator—the "temps du discours." In a significant distinction they group in a first subdivision the three tenses mentioned—the perfect, the imperfect, and the present—and relegate to a second division others such as the past historic and the pluperfect. Ducrot and Todorov summarize their reasoning by proposing that the first subdivision is linked and subordinate to the narrator's own present time, whereas the second assumes an objective chronology which only associates the events one with another.

In fact, they quite innocently confirm just how coherent is Ramuz's choice of tenses in a narrative which repeatedly shows the characteristics of speech, rather than those of conventional writing, where the "codified intention" of the speaker is the determining factor.[66] In Ramuz's novels the preferred tenses are inseparable from the "présent de l'énonciation" which imposes the dominant temporality; thus the events of the story are increasingly conveyed by the perfect, imperfect, and present tenses to *attach,* but also to *subordinate,* the action related to the present of the narrator. Beyond the relativity and anteriority of tense the accent is placed firmly on the present, the verbal form which is best suited to the expression of permanent existence.

Throughout the novels Ramuz evidences a great awareness of the complex values of the different tenses. A particularly fine sense of distinction is to be found in *Derborence* at the moment when Victorine begins to dream of Antoine:

And he [Antoine], he would say: "A little kiss, just one . . ."
She would say: "Where?"—"On the corner of my eye."
"No," she would say, "because first I have something to tell you. Turn your face upwards and I shall put my head flat, like that you won't prick me any more. And like that I shall have your ear right next to my mouth, its because of the secret. Antoine . . ."
She turned over again in the big bed and the hours of the night began to pass. Perhaps she had drowsed a little.
There must have been a bit of a storm.
He was saying: "This secret, what is it? Is it money? Is it a visit?"
She was saying: "Guess!"
The storm was continuing. The noise, which had begun in her dream, slips softly into reality. She opens her eyes, she hears it still.

Et lui [Antoine], il dirait: "Un petit baiser, rien qu'un . . ."
Elle dirait: "Où?"—"Sur le pâle de l'oeil."
"Non," dirait-t-elle, "parce que j'ai d'abord quelque chose à te dire. Tourne ta figure en l'air, moi je mets ma tête à plat, comme ça tu ne piqueras plus. Et comme ça j'aurai ton oreille tout près de ma bouche, c'est à cause du secret. Antoine . . ."
Elle s'est retournée encore dans le grand lit et les heures de la nuit commençaient à passer. Peut-être qu'elle s'était assoupie.
Il a dû faire un peu d'orage.
Lui disait: "Ce secret, qu'est-ce que c'est? C'est de l'argent? C'est une visite?"
Elle disait: "Devine!"
Il continuait à faire de l'orage. Le bruit, qui avait commencé dans son rêve, glisse tout doucement à la réalité. Elle ouvre les yeux, elle l'entend toujours.[67]

As Victorine's mind moves from simple meditation through a moment of dream towards her awakening, the changing levels of consciousness are admirably approximated by the chosen tenses. The initial conditionals—"dirait"—slip into the more definite imperfect—"disait"—as the character falls asleep and mere wish becomes the conviction of dream. Meanwhile, the perfect tense translates the external facts. However, the storm is both external and internal at the same time—"avait commencé dans son rêve"— and thus appears in both the perfect and imperfect tenses. Finally, the present tense by its contrast with the imperfect of the dream world announces a return to waking reality. Such an interweaving of tenses shows how skillfully Ramuz was able to handle his vehicle and, moreover, that for him the force of the different tenses was not solely, nor even principally, temporal.

Indeed, on other occasions he goes still further and, by juxtaposing a tense and a particular adverb, he succeeds in re-valuing the tense, the normal temporality of which is no longer operative. For example, in those cases where the expression "à présent," or less strikingly "maintenant," is attached to a verb in the past, it is no longer possible to apply normal tense notions, for the temporality does not depend on the verb but on the deictic form in question (Jakobson's "embrayeur"). Here is a typical case taken from La Grande Peur dans la montagne:

He [Barthélemy] was surprised to hear the glacier, and it was at present as if the glacier were coughing, whilst Barthélemy continued under the strangely-colored sky.

Il [Barthélemy] s'étonnait d'entendre le glacier, et c'était à présent comme si le glacier toussait, tandis que Barthélemy allait sous une couleur de ciel étonnante.[68]

In this passage the narrative verb "c'était" is past but the sensibility of the collective narrator is present—"à présent." By this effect where the imperfect is deprived of its full verbal force Ramuz invokes not only the "Person," for to borrow once again an expression of Ducrot and Todorov "le référent ne peut être déterminé que par rapport aux interlocuteurs",[69] but also a notion of Time that transcends the fragmentation of accepted grammatical tense usage.

Despite the delicate ingenuity of the foregoing it would be unwise to attempt to reduce all the variations to a law or a single system. On many occasions the formal rules of sequence are broken and the critic is obliged to yield to the conviction of Brunot that "le chapitre de la concordance des temps se résume en une ligne: il n'y en a pas."

There are other times, too, when it is likely that the reader will arrive at a better appreciation of Ramuz's world by deferring any fragmented judgment. If the value of the tenses in certain passages no longer depends on temporal or psychological relativity, then a global perception of the events being related, beyond the individual tenses, will tend to resituate the action on that atemporal level towards which much of Ramuz's narrative technique converges. Certainly, the tense changes in a passage like the one which follows seem to defy any grammatical or even psychological analysis and, thereby, confirm the complete devaluation of independent tense significance:

There was water in plentiful supply: There has been more then enough wine in two barrels which had been brought by the pack-mule. First they had rested, while eating and drinking, as the cows had begun immediately to graze; then the men in groups had been to examine the repairs in the room where the cheese is made, and in the one for sleeping; then in the part which serves as a shelter, in case of bad weather, for the herd; they had found everything in order, there was nothing to say, now it was once again a fine strong chalet, just what was needed;—then some of them had been for a stroll in the pasture, while the mules were being unloaded and the tools being put in position.
The boys and the girls were seated in groups on the grass; there has been some more drinking, then some dancing.
They were dancing, they were going to drink between dances; the boys and the girls were dancing and drinking, the men were drinking. And they too had drunk and had danced.

Il y avait de l'eau en suffisance: il y a eu du vin plus qu'en suffisance dans deux tonnelets qui avaient été apportés par le mulet aux provisions. D'abord on s'était reposé, tout en mangeant et en buvant, tandis que tout de suite les vaches s'étaient mises à pâtre; puis les hommes par groupes avaient été examiner les réparations dans la pièce où on fait le fromage, et dans celle où on couche; puis dans la partie qui sert d'abri, en cas de mauvais temps, pour le troupeau; ils avaient trouvé tout en place; il n'y avait pas à dire, c'était de nouveau maintenant un bel et bon chalet, tout ce qu'il y a de plus suffisant;—ensuite quelques-uns d'entre eux avaient été faire un tour dans le pâturage, pendant qu'on déchargeait les mulets et on mettait en place les ustensiles.
Les garçons et les filles étaient assis par groupes dans l'herbe; on a bu encore, puis on a dansé.
On dansait, on allait boire entre les danses; les garçons et les filles dansaient et buvaient, les hommes buvaient. Et eux aussi avaient bu et avaient dansé.[70]

Most narratives mix their tenses—one has only to consider Chateaubriand for whom Ramuz never lost his enthusiasm—but the tenses in the above passage refuse adequate individual exegesis. The dynamic fusion of once distinct time-indicators is one of the most remarkable and widespread characteristics of Ramuz's novels.

To this unsettling chronological confusion—or rather fusion—is added a temporal amplification which results from the accumulation of forms and allusions endowed with historical overtones. In this respect Ramuz again shows that, far from being a solitary, he is closely aligned with other authors—with Thomas Mann for whom the omnitemporality of events is a fundamental notion, with James Joyce who in *Ulysses*, from his title onwards, makes systematic use of symbolic reference, and with André Malraux, a few years later, who creates a vast trans-historical backdrop in both *L'Espoir* and *Les Noyers de l'Altenburg*. The ambition of all of these is to effect an exemplary synthesis of the theme Man.

Ramuz, for example, accumulates expressions—rare today—such as "les aller rejoindre," "n'y pas venir," "dût-il," expressions the use of which extends far back into time and recalls the classical phrasing of centuries past. Elsewhere, he prefers the form "s'asseoit" to "s'assied," thus prolonging the period with which his language must be associated. In *La Grande Peur dans la montagne* we read:

Pont qui a rejoint le garde, s'asseoit, ôte d'abord ses souliers qu'il jette loin de lui, puis le pantalon de toile, jette le pantalon de toile qui tombe à côté des souliers; ôte ses gants.

Pont who has rejoined the guard sits down, takes off first of all his shoes which he throws a long way off, then the canvas trousers, throws down the canvas trousers which land next to the shoes; takes off his gloves.[71]

Littré informs us that the "oi" form ("eoi" by contagion with the infinitive), unusual in contemporary French, is of ancient, provincial origin:

The two conjugations, "j'assieds" and "j'assois," are the trace of two provincial pronunciations which were frequent in old French: "j'assois" in the center, "j'assieds" in the west.[72]

For similar reasons Ramuz elects to use "être couru" rather than "avoir couru":

they had run from the hayshed with their guns, intending to prevent his passing.[73]

ils étaient courus hors du fenil avec leurs fusils, pensant l'empêcher de passer.

The form with "être" is correct but "peu usitée" according to Littré, who insists, however, that "dans l'ancienne langue il [être] était de plein usage."[74] Robert confirms that "*courir a été employé avec l'auxiliare être*" and in particular he cites the period of Madame de Sévigné and Racine.[75]

As we have stated, the tendency of this language, both popular and archaic, is to detach itself from any precise setting and to convey, in its turn, that same conception of permanence which results from the variations in tense.

Worthy of at least passing reference is another device which functions towards the same end, and which has been closely examined by A. Praplan in an article, "Ramuz et la Bible," which appeared in *Europe* in 1967. There Praplan explains how, by approximations of the Biblical tone and a widespread network of analogy and reference to Scriptural events and characters, Ramuz sought to present the Swiss cantons as an integral and exemplary part of human experience:

The Vaudois writer will try to insert the soil and the country folk of his own region in the intemporal *duration* of the Bible. In his way he nourished a desire for an epic poem, both pastoral and Biblical, of which each narration would be a fragment.[76]

Without wishing to repeat Praplan's detailed findings, let me merely acknowledge my similar conviction that in Ramuz the particularized importance of the events being narrated diminishes in the light of a Biblical world that provides an omnipresent connective tissue of universality of which the Vaudois and Valaisan incidents are no more than a recent dramatization—"a fragment."

There is, too, an element of Swiss origin which contributes to the historical dilation we are considering and which functions in the same way as those of the Bible. The Rhône, without which this part of my survey would be incomplete, is a frequent backcloth in the three novels we are discussing and always evokes an aura of permanence:

in the very depth of the night, the Rhône. One deep uninterrupted voice, one vast breath.[77]
The noise it [the Rhône] makes is a continuous noise.[78]
But from its depths [the valley's] which remained hidden, a message

nevertheless came to you, that is a voice, recounting endlessly an old story
never completed and perhaps never begun: it is the Rhône that one could
not see, it is the Rhône that one could hear.

Because it has always been there and from time immemorial it murmurs
there.[79]

In the first two quotations the Rhône is seen temporarily as a
symbol of continuity ("uninterrupted", "continuous") but is extended in the third to suggest eternity itself ("always"). This voice
which murmurs "from time immemorial" is intoning the fundamental message of Ramuz, for whom the Rhône watercourse, despite the
irregularities of its winding itinerary, is as unceasing as the history of
Man.

IX *The Creative Essence*

My attempts to define the mature Ramuzian technique have
clearly been facilitated by the author's unceasing willingness to
comment on his artistic progress at the very moment of creation. It
is this same concomitant lucidity which will now allow us, through a
final examination of those devices, so deceptively discreet in their
novelistic guise but which abound in *La Grande Peur dans la montagne, Farinet,* and *Derborence,* to determine with exactitude the
precise nature of this universal and permanent element in Man on
which I have repeatedly insisted.

I have previously alluded to Ramuz's disregard for the fabled
beauty of the Alps. There is for him an important distinction between the attitude of the tourist and that of the inhabitant towards
the same landscape, which for the latter is not in any way admired as
"picturesque" but experienced intimately. Rather than a source of
enchantment and *rêverie*, for those who live there the mountain
constitutes primarily the place where nature manifests itself at the
height of its violence and instability. Even without elaborating on
the severe rigors of a singularly inhospitable climate, one cannot but
admit that the mortal danger of the cliffs and the glaciers makes the
mountain-dweller's experience into one of those "extreme situa-
tions" that characterize so much European literature of the first
three decades of the century. But, Ramuz's mountain, extreme by
its cataclysmic aspect, yet free of the quasi-exoticism of a Malraux or
a Conrad, by virtue of the insistent presence of the everyday, may
well reflect reality in a more complete and exemplary way.

In *Besoin de grandeur* Ramuz describes in full the enormity of the destructive force which seems to animate these upper regions of the earth where the immense difficulties of human existence are crystallized:

it [the mountain] is only ruins and rockfalls, not only ruining itself, but ruining all it encounters on its way [. . .]. Here in these mountains nothing which does not yield to the rule of the strongest. The rockface falls into the pasture slips into the torrent [. . .]. We are consoled too easily, we laud too willingly our mountains which are merely the image of our damnation. They only predict our end.[80]

If the mountain tends downwards, the aspirations of man proceed steadfastly in the other direction; the very expressions "aspiration" and "elevation," so frequent in life and poetry, suggest a movement upwards and indicate immediately the inevitability of the opposition that must develop. It is therefore not surprising that Ramuz, in order to impose his vision of Man *the creator*, incorporates with remarkable frequency into his narration, at privileged moments, the key situation of an ascent—"une montée."

In a mountainous region man's movement necessarily takes place along a more or less vertical axis—both downwards and upwards. What is certain is that Ramuz's novels emphasize in particular the ascending movement and relegate to an incidental position, or even reject totally, the descents. Gilbert Guisan observes, for example, that in the later editions of *Derborence* the final descent of Thérèse and Antoine, which figured in the original edition, has been suppressed. Such a modification places in a terminal position and, therefore, in greater relief the significance of their miraculous climb upwards—that slow approach which reunites for ever a couple temporarily separated by the avalanche.

It is certain that Ramuz was fully conscious of the potential "mystical" value of these ascents, beyond any question of athleticism or physical courage, for he has often commented on the links he discerns between spatial elevation and a corresponding interior elevation. It may be, for example, an ascent towards God:

The mountain for many of those who frequent it is a pretext for escape. Is it only that? Are there not too those who contemplate, for whom action scarcely counts, for whom action is only a means and a physical means for an "elevation," the word having two meanings which here coincide?

I am thinking of those religious spirits for whom physical elevation is little more than the symbol of another elevation. They climb very high, they climb high into the snow and travel for a long time across the glaciers until they finally reach some peak of difficult access where they set themselves up, two or three, or even alone, with their pipe. They dominate [. . .]. They contemplate at present the world from above and contemplate from above the work of God; nothing separates them any longer from him who is present above his work.[81]

But the role of God is extremely limited in the Swiss author's universe. For Ramuz the "montées" are rather symptomatic of a need for fulfillment, that is to say of a yearning for perfection (in an etymological sense for the peasant), for an *absolute*, perhaps mystical, probably poetic, but definitely stripped of any conventional divinity. Appropriately, Ramuz's own itinerary was seen as not dissimilar to that of a man climbing a mountain: "perhaps sometime I shall arrive at that lofty place, from where everything reveals itself and where the reason for everything is seen."[82]

The mountain ascents, therefore, would seem to permit not only an evocation of the estate of man, but, at the same time, of the perpetual tendency of the poet. They may well reveal, in addition to the eternal struggle which is inherent in the human condition, the difficulty and the miracle of artistic creation.

It would have been possible, in order to distill the essential qualities of these ascents, to have examined any one of a very large number—some thirteen major passages in the three novels in question (*La Grande Peur dans la montagne*, pp. 14–24, 47–51, 191–200, 237–240; *Farinet*, pp. 12–15, 65–67, 122–124, 235–237; *Derborence*, pp. 29–32, 115–121, 173–181, 208–218, 222–226.)

An analysis of any one of these—with perhaps the first ascent of Joseph in *La Grande Peur dans la montagne* as the most exemplary—would expose certain elements which seem to characterize for Ramuz at this terminal point in his evolution the essence of the human condition. In each he evokes the *difficulty* and *solitude* of the journey, the *effort* required and yet the joy of *accomplishment* which colors the vision which so often awaits the climber. In Ramuz's works the perilous and exhausting ascent of the mountain-dweller reflects the painful creative effort of man—peasant or poet; the description of a task fulfilled reveals equally the common experience of all.

But the significance of these ascents is not yet exhausted, for it is not merely a question of the aspiration of a potential creator, but of the moment of creation itself. By his presence and by his movement, the peasant invests with life that which surrounds him; he acts and causes to react. His ascent does not only constitute a symbol of the creative effort, but is also a fertile source of poetry. He is an energizing force which animates the inanimate and, in transforming, gives birth.

The physical presence of a man ascending generates necessarily, by the normal laws of perspective, the corollary of an apparent reciprocal movement by the surrounding objects; as the man changes position, so the things regroup. Moreover, on account of the ruggedness of the terrain, any mountain ascent is an act of defiance, the enormity of which is often understood by the climber, whence the considerable emotion—joy or fear—which he manifests. This emotion, too, seems to invest with life objects which would otherwise be inert. Let us first consider the peasant's physical presence.

For Ramuz, it is a fallacy to evoke an objective reality which exists independently of man; external reality only exists as a function of man, it is inseparable from the presence of an observer. When man is absent, things appear cold and dead: "behind those who were coming, and as they were coming, the valley moved into silence, into cold and into death."[83]

The lack of life and animation in the surroundings is a direct result in *Derborence* of the departure of Antoine and Thérèse. It was from them that the objects took their only existence. In identical fashion in *La Grande Peur dans la montagne*, the disappearance of Victorine reacts on the Alpine landscape and returns it to oblivion: "Because she is no longer, nothing is any longer. All was empty, all was deserted at the same time as it grew cold and it grew deeply silent."[84]

In Ramuz the importance of a human presence may be reduced without falsification to the presence of an eye, for if other poets are often musicians, activated above all by sound, Ramuz is the visual poet par excellence. It is from the peasant eye—a virgin eye, let me insist, untutored by knowledgeable society—that Ramuz's poetry springs and that is effected the transformation of objective reality which may well be the very definition of creativity:

On dit que Besson prend avec les yeux les choses qui sont et les arrange, de sorte qu'elles sont à nouveaux, et elles sont les mêmes et sont autrement.

They say that Besson takes with his eyes things which are and arranges them, in such a way that they are anew, and they are the same and are differently.[85]

Just as did Besson in *Le Passage du poète*, just as do the protagonists of each of the major novels, so does the poet reorganize the world *prelogically* by reversing the established, informed, order. For him the verb "voir" means precisely the opposite of "savoir," since for the naïve onlooker the phenomenon precedes its explanation. Once again, the description of an ascending movement proves revealing; for, in those passages, it becomes especially clear that Ramuz presents an immediate, non-rationalized, perception. Henceforth, grouped around the man journeying upwards, it is the objects which move, which shift position in a super-Proustian ballet, which resituate themselves; only subsequent reflection exposes the relativity of this effect. The external world only exists for Ramuz as a retinal image, in the eye of a person whose every movement will modify the appearance of the world.

In *La Grande Peur dans la montagne*, on the occasion of the visit of the five men to the pasturage, the ascent is filtered through an observer at one with the villagers:

We ["On"] began to climb. We gradually moved away from the torrent which streamed down on our left, while we climbed on the right, among the humps of ground which came forward and crossed your path, so that it was necessary to go down again, then we began climbing once more. We passed in front of a small cluster of haysheds which watched you come, falling silent to watch you come after which, they huddled together, as if to tell each other things.[86]

Ramuz sketches here, at different stages of the journey, the narrator's continually changing associations with the objects encountered along the route. The verbs of action which are attached to otherwise inanimate things create a new world—where the "torrent" becomes an Alpinist, the "humps" prepare to attack and the "haysheds" cluster together in conversation.

In *Derborence* it is the chalets and, again, the stream which lose their immobility because of the dynamic presence of Thérèse and her companions:

We ["On"] had finished by rejoining the torrent which at first flowed in the depths below you; but it climbs to you little by little and finally it is at the same level. They walked in this way for a long time, then a first chalet is seen. It is built on the right of the path in the middle of a square of field which is dominated by the forest, itself dominated by rocks. We advance a little further; and a second chalet shows itself, then three, then four, similarly poor and tiny.[87]

The gradual elevation of the mountain stream, together with the entrance of the four chalets, are the normal results of the laws of perspective; but in the Ramuzian universe the link which denotes the dependence and relativity of the apparent movement of an object is omitted, and the passive becomes active.

The physical presence of a man brings with it inevitably a sensibility, that is, an emotional presence which is also capable of giving force to the outside world. He who finds himself alone on a mountain, face to face with the immensity of nature, discovers that his state of mind—even of his body, alert or weary—influences his perception of the objects through which he journeys. Since, in a Ramuzian novel, every ascent is filtered through a character, or else an anonymous *but related* companion, the reality described will no longer be a collection of elements enumerated by the intelligence and distinct from the observer, but will be seen as an affective adjustment of objective reality.

Maurice Merleau-Ponty, in a lecture delivered in 1945 at the Institut des Hautes Etudes Cinématographiques, explains that sensation and perception are a single act and that intellectualization is subsequent. The immediate perception is global and unconscious; it is only retrospectively that we establish relationships and patterns between things. He claims that it is necessary to go back beyond intelligence to rediscover authentic perception: "Perception is not a sort of incipient knowledge and a first exercise of the intelligence, we must discover a relationship with the world and a presence in the world which is older than intelligence."[88]

These words of a phenomenologist, which in the circumstances were intended to apply above all to the perception of film, are equally valid for Ramuz's poetry. This "relationship with the world" and this "presence in the world" which must be "older than intelligence" are those of the countryman-narrator, who never rationalizes an environment which organizes itself spontaneously around him, but who, unknowingly, animates and colors it according to the emotion or sensation of the moment.

The Alpine element which is the most revealing in this respect is undoubtedly the glacier, and its frequent reappearance at decisive moments emphasizes that, for Ramuz, it constitutes perhaps the most remarkable of all natural phenomena. Thus, in a passage taken from *La Grande Peur dans la montagne*, the glacier, despite its virtual geophysical immobility, seems to rise up and advance in opposition to the temerity of Joseph:

Puis, en retour vers vous, venait le glacier. [. . .]. C'était dresse, en même temps que ça tombait; ça venait vers en bas en même temps que c'était immobile: une cascade de mille mètres et plus, changée en pierre, mais ayant encore ses remous, ses bouillonnements, ses surplombs, ses élans en avant, ses brisements, ses repos; et, enfin, dans le bas, elle reprenait sa course.

Tout le glacier qui était là, ayant barré le chemin à Joseph, alors Joseph renverse encore la tête, il la ramène vers en bas, il la renverse de nouveau; et de nouveau venait cette énorme chose pas vraie, qu'on ne pouvait pas comprendre, ne produisant rien, ne servant à rien, comme si on était arrivé au bout de la vie, au bout du monde, au bout du monde et de la vie.[89]

then, closer to you, came the glacier, [. . .] it was rearing upwards, at the same time as it was falling; it was coming downwards at the same time as it was motionless; a cascade of a thousand meters and more, changed into stone, but still having its swirls, its bubbles, its projections, its jagged bits, its breaks, its pauses; and, finally, at the bottom, it resumed its course. . .].

The whole glacier which was there, having barred the path to Joseph, then Joseph tilts back his head further, he lowers it, he tilts it once more; and again there came this enormous unbelievable thing, that one couldn't understand, not producing anything, not serving any purpose, as if one had reached the end of life, the end of the world, the end of the world and of life.

From the beginning of the passage the eye of the narrating character is fixed on the glacier, the appearance of which is conditioned by the psychological state of this lone spectator. The extreme tension of this moment high up on the mountain directs the narrator's glance towards the most dangerous point and imposes a movement on nature—"venait," "dressé," "tombait," "venait vers en bas." The glacier also becomes physically hostile to the point where it seems ready to leap at him—"dressé"—like some gigantic predator. The glacier again reveals an inimical quality by its an-

tagonistic attitude in *Derborence*, an attitude evident to Antoine as
he studies the route traced by the avalanche which had entombed
him. For Antoine the path of the falling glacier seemed so well
calculated, it was "as if it had aimed for us."[90]

Even if the dominant human sentiment, when confronted by this
terrifying potential power, is most often fear, joy too, at times, will
release a latent force. In *Farinet* the hero glories in his new-found
freedom, and his delight even rebounds onto the glaciers:

perhaps that's it, freedom, he thinks and that's pleasure, because an opening has suddenly appeared in the emptiness; and there just in front of him,
just at his level, in the blue, all those glaciers intertwined together were like
a bouquet of roses wrapped in white paper.[91]

The ecstasy of this moment of revelation seems to communicate
itself to the glaciers, which embrace each other with a rare warmth
and fraternity.

Certainly, the movement generated by happiness is less violent,
less vigorous, than that to be found in the episodes describing fear;
there is often little more than a friendly greeting. Again, *La Grande
Peur dans la montagne* furnishes an example:

Et, dans le fond du pâturage, venait aussi le glacier, qui pendait là, peint en
belles couleurs de même que toute la combe; et ces belles couleurs toutes
ensemble leur venaient contre.[92]

And, at the bottom of the pasture, there came too the glacier, which was
hanging there, painted in beautiful colors as was all the valley; and these
beautiful colors all together came towards them.

The enthusiasm of the five men who, after their arduous climb,
discover the practicability of the pasturage, reaches out to their very
surroundings. Again the glacier, elsewhere so threatening, seems to
deck itself out for their arrival, comes to meet them—"venait aussi le
glacier"—with a languorous movement—"pendait." This mountain
welcome, this colorful and active beauty, reflects the new confidence of the peasants. And as is often the case, the poetic animation
of objects encountered by the climber is complemented by a light-
ing or a coloring which illuminates still more the creative force of
the protagonist.

Despite its somewhat cursory nature,[93] this investigation of the
passages describing ascents shows adequately, I feel, Ramuz's idea

of man climbing painfully upwards, man striving towards a vision of communion, man capable of transforming the world, Man the Maker. Valaisan mountain-dweller, Biblical peasant, or Vaudois poet, all are capable of the same experience, each possesses his own creative capacity. Yet, the poet-writer is not only amongst those that have this universal human essence, he is also by his particular *métier* the one who must find an appropriate formulation of the experience. In putting pen to paper Ramuz informs and concretizes his message—and in his best novels the integrity of his vision and expression is absolute.

CHAPTER 4

Conclusion: From the Top
of the Mountain

I A Time to Remember

THE stature that Ramuz now justly enjoyed in much of Europe in the wake of those artistic achievements examined in the previous chapter, crowned as it had been by literary prizes, requests to collaborate, and the applause of new enthusiasts, brought with it too the not altogether unusual wish to step back and survey. Heralded by his offerings in *Aujourd'hui*, a journal created for him in 1929 as a personal mouthpiece by his great benefactor Mermod, and confirmed by a further rich assortment of comments in innumerable periodicals—often under pseudonyms that happily invoke his fictional landscape, Maurice Devenoge, Jean Lavallaz, Auguste Pittet, Constant Pollier—it was now the twilight age of reflections and memoirs.

Neither bourgeois nor capitalist, neither radical nor liberal, it was Ramuz's intransigent independence of mind that was to make the fruit of his long meditation so significant. Of little interest, even facile, as a social or political commentator, it is rather as a sort of contemporary religious humanist in a world devoid of revealed divinity, but charged with the force of man's own creative capacity, that he assumes his true dimension. It was not without justification that Jean Paulhan wrote to Ramuz on 6 May 1934 "C'est de vous que le monde a terriblement besoin."[1]

Few lives allow themselves to be compartmentalized totally, and the Vaudois novelist's is no exception; for the first of the later meditations, *Une main*, was published a year before *Derborence*. The creator and the philosopher are only artifically separated. Indeed, the accident which occasioned the month of inactivity which engendered *Une main* in fact took place as early as December 1930, when Ramuz slipped on a frozen surface and broke his humerus. It is this

121

misfortune which is described with great precision at the com-
mencement of the work in question, before the subsequent rich
synthesis of his art and his life takes over the text. The description of
a personal experience becomes a reflection on time and ultimately
on the nature of man's greatness: "I see that the true link is between
what one is and what is, in the contact of man in his totality with the
object in its totality (and thereafter if possible to manage to communicate this contact)."[2]

These considerations are further clarified in a second work, *Taille
de l'homme*. There, as he himself indicates in an enlightening pro-
spective publicity blurb which he had forwarded to Henri Mermod,
the merit of Ramuz's meditation becomes especially clear in the
light of current circumstances:

The author deals with various questions that events have caused to become
of immediate importance. He examines in particular the representation that
man has been brought to make of himself, in the face of a universe that
recent scientific discoveries have infinitely enlarged. Has man definitely
renounced all anthropomorphism? The old solutions that had been brought
to the problem by pagan religion as well as Christian religion, is he going to
abandon them totally? As for that proposed by materialist communism, and
which is of a new type, since for it human life takes place entirely on one
level, what are its chances? and in what does it betray men? in what does it
betray even the science on which it claims to depend?[3]

It is to this discussion of his vision of contemporary man, a man
seemingly lost in a world where the onetime pillars of the Church
and Science are no longer steady and have yet adequately to be
replaced, that Ramuz's artistic itinerary has brought him. What was
felt intuitively and informed poetically, is now to be rationalized and
annotated directly.

Throughout, the dominant tone is one of anguish as Ramuz
unflinchingly dismisses the different myths, old and new; there is no
longer a system which fixes men solidly in the world around them:
"The real drama is that man no longer has any stature, being without
common measure with the material universe, and, on the level of
his consciousness, without any links in a world where he can
nowhere rediscover that stature."[4]

There is only general indifference: the drama is that the universe no longer appears to us as anything other than a monstrous
assemblage of elements indifferent to themselves and to us."[5] In this

invertebrate, disjointed, world neither communism—a faith which isolates man in a painful void—nor science, in its new destructive guise, is an adequate consolation. The need of contemporary man is now stated unequivocally as the rediscovery of that total communion which is innate in the unsophisticated countryman of yesteryear. What clearer rationalization and, indeed, justification of Ramuz's narratives could there be!

These published versions of stages in a continuing Ramuzian reflection saw a third added some two years later with the appearance of *Questions*. The situation of man becomes rather more dramatically the situation of the artist and, ultimately, or perhaps initially—so coherent is Ramuz's vision—the Vaudois writer's own.

Before reuniting them under the all-embracing notion of art, Ramuz does linger too on a marginal distinction between poet and painter. He admits willingly his own predilection for painting and its position as a key to his own literature: "It did happen alas! that I wrote books, but it is not my true 'métier.' My education has been effected by the painters."[6]

He then goes on to emphasize that literature, as opposed to painting, suffers from a lamentable tradition by which the public wishes, even demands, to *understand* and to receive answers: "I should like to excite, nothing more, but only the painters have the right to excite and nothing more."[7] or elsewhere: "from him [the writer] answers are expected whereas he is happy to put questions."

He conjectures finally on a satisfactory definition of the true artist—poet or painter—and it does not seem in any way surprising that the expressions he proposes evoke simply a man creating with love, joy, and sincerity—expressions that could readily embrace too that most fundamental of Ramuzian personages, the countryman: "Isn't the artist, when all's said and done, simply the man who expresses himself totally and fully in his work, because into it he puts his whole being, including his upper parts; that is the pleasure he finds in it, that is the love he brings to it."[9]

It is surely at this point, with the closing pages of *Questions*, that Ramuz's lifelong meditation on man's creativity reaches its apogee, explaining, justifying, and crowning the great works of fiction.

II   *A House in Order*

The ten years which remained to Ramuz, cut through by a second European holocaust, were not to be characterized by the same remarkable and original impetus. Apart from a series of more or less autobiographical studies, interesting for what they reveal of Ramuz but not intrinsically—one should mention *Paris, notes d'un Vaudois, Découverte du monde, René Auberjonois*—and two sadly undistinguished novels, *Si le soleil ne revenait pas* and *La Guerre aux papiers*, the most memorable event was the author's own preparation of his *Oeuvres complètes*.

These, requested by Mermod, were first announced early in 1940 and required an extended laborious effort from an elderly man no longer in the best of health. The problem of the right of the mature artist to redress and correct the errors and weaknesses of the young muse is a considerable one, and one which undoubtedly caused Ramuz many misgivings. However, the definitive edition was finally ready, late in 1941; and the novelist's letters of that time indicate not only relief at his deliverance from so onerous a task, but also joy at his own success in having polished awkwardnesses, without plunging into substantial, disruptive, and possibly, "dishonest" changes.[10]

But, inevitably, an unrelenting pursuit of excellence in his chosen expression was now increasingly taking its toll on a body that had never been of the strongest. The years 1945, 1946, and 1947 saw repeated visits to clinics for the treatment of stones, before the final illness which was only terminated by the author's death on 23 May 1947.

Only someone totally insensitive to Ramuz's poetry could ever choose to question the report that was circulated of his last moments, of the peaceful and contented murmuring with which he left this life, "Bien, bien, bien . . ."—for his quest, as exhaustive and exhausting as that of any artist before him, had been most wonderfully fulfilled.

Notes and References

Chapter One

1. *Découverte du monde*, p. 51. (As indicated in the "Preface" in each case the translations are my own; the details of the original text are given in the bibliography.)
2. *Ibid.*, p. 132.
3. *Ibid.*, p. 41.
4. *Ibid.*, p. 153.
5. *Ibid.*, p. 163.
6. *Ibid.*, p. 79.
7. *Ibid.*, p. 166.
8. *Journal*, p. 70.
9. *Ibid.*, p. 24.
10. *Ibid.*, pp. 30–31.
11. *Ibid.*, p. 37.
12. *Ibid.*, p. 73.
13. *Ibid.*, pp. 51–52.
14. *Ibid.*, p. 77.
15. *Découverte du monde*, p. 208.
16. *Ibid.*, p. 208.
17. *Journal*, p. 77.
18. P. Godet, *La Bibliothèque universelle*, December, 1903.
19. F. Chavannes, *Gazette de Lausanne*, November 19, 1903.
20. J. Cougnard, *La Patrie suisse*, December 30, 1903.
21. G. Vallette, *La Suisse*, November 13, 1903.
22. *Oeuvres complètes*, I, p. 37.
23. *Journal*, p. 94.
24. *Ibid.*, p. 96.
25. G. Guisan (ed.), *C.-F. Ramuz, ses amis et son temps*, I, Lausanne, Bibliothèque des Arts, 1967, p. 121.
26. P. Godet, *La Bibliothèque universelle*, April 1904.
27. G. Guisan (ed.), *op. cit.*, p. 128.
28. *Ibid.*, p. 146.

29. *Journal*, p. 108.

30. *Découverte du monde*, pp. 208–209.

31. *Aline*, p. 47.

32. *Ibid.*, p. 54.

33. *Ibid.*, p. 58.

34. *Ibid.*, p. 117.

35. *Ibid.*, p. 12. ". . . et puis elle attendait de mourir à son heure, car Dieu est juste, et on ne va pas contre sa volonté."

36. G. Guisan (ed.), *op. cit.*, II, p. 95.

37. *Ibid.*, p. 97.

38. *Ibid.*, p. 107.

39. *Journal*, p. 128.

40. Anne-Marie Monnet, Prix Fémina 1945, who shared Cécile Cellier's studio at this time, reveals much about Ramuz's life in Paris in her recollections published in the review *Adam*, London, 1967.

41. *Journal*, p. 123.

42. G. Guisan (ed.) *op.cit.*, II, p. 171.

43. B. Grivel, *Gazette de Lausanne*, December 22, 1905.

44. *Oeuvres complètes*, I, p. 190.

45. *Oeuvres complètes*, II, p. 362.

46. P. Seippel, *Journal de Genève*, June 16, 1907.

47. *Journal*, p. 126.

48. *Ibid.*, pp. 143, 147, 149.

49. B. Voyenne, *C.-F.Ramuz et la sainteté de la terre*, Neuchâtel, La Baconnière, 1967, pp. 30–31.

50. M. Zermatten, *Ramuz à Lens*, Bienne, Panorama, 1967, p. 12.

51. *Oeuvres complètes*, XVIII, p. 232.

52. *Journal*, p. 155.

53. *Jean-Luc persécuté*, p. 69.

54. G. Guisan (ed.), *op.cit.*, IV. p. 25.

55. *Lettres 1900–1918*, p. 210.

56. G. Vallette, *La Semaine littéraire*, November 28, 1908.

57. E. Marsan, *Le Divan*, January, 1909.

58. G. Guisan (ed.), *op.cit.*, IV. p. 97.

59. *Lettres 1900–1918*, p. 222.

60. G. Guisan (ed.), *op.cit.*, IV, p. 66.

61. *Journal*, p. 167.

62. *Aimé Pache, peintre vaudois*, p. 18.

63. *Ibid.*, pp. 46–47.

"Elle s'était remise à tresser ses couronnes.

Aimé s'asseyait sur le banc. Elle à côté de lui avec un vieux caraco bleu, une jupe tout effrangée, et ses doigts étaient noirs comme des morceaux de boix mort.

Mais ils étaient habiles et doux dans la mousse et les pâquettes, qu'ils assemblaient avec délicatesse; ils bougeaient doucement; ils se levaient un peu en l'air, comme au jeu de marionettes, avec au bout les petits bouquets roses qu'ils attachaient d'une ficelle, et puis de ficelle en ficelle, tout autour du cercle d'osier;—un petit ouvrage bien propre."

64. *Ibid.*, p. 247. "Il y a une résurrection. Il y a en nous des forces de vie. Elles nous poussent à mourir souvent, mais à ressortir de la mort, elles nous font mourir pour nous faire mieux vivre.

Il était sorti, ce soir-là, et était monté à travers les bois, jusqu'à un lieu nommé Sauges d'où on domine tout le pays."

65. *Ibid.*, p. 250.

66. *Ibid.*, pp. 251–252.

67. *Ibid.*, p. 254.

68. *Lettres 1900–1918*, p. 227.

69. G. Guisan (ed.), *op. cit.*, IV, p. 141.

70. *Ibid.*, V., p. 39.

71. *Journal*, p. 167.

72. *Ibid.*, p. 179.

73. *Ibid.*, p. 180.

74. *Lettres 1900–1918*, p. 284.

75. A. Béguin, *Patience de Ramuz*, Neuchâtel, La Baconnière, 1950, p. 64.

76. *Vie de Samuel Belet*, p. 9.

77. *Ibid.*, p. 136.

78. *Ibid.*, p. 144.

79. *Ibid.*, p. 288.

80. *Ibid.*, p. 290.

81. M. Muret, *Journal de débats*, June 8, 1913.

82. G. Guisan (ed.), *op. cit.*, V, p. 64.

Chapter Two

1. *Lettres 1900–1918*, p. 296.

2. G. Guisan (ed.), *op.cit.*, p. 124.

3. *Oeuvres complètes*, VII, pp. 57–58.

4. *Ibid.*, VI, p. 74.

5. *Ibid.*, p. 73.

6. After this first number the Cahiers continued through 34 volumes, and were complemented by various artistic manifestations, lectures, exhibitions, dramatic and musical productions. A full history of them can be found in the *Gazette de Lausanne*, May 31, 1947.

7. *Oeuvres complètes*, VII, p. 13.

8. *Ibid.*, p. 13.

9. *Ibid.*, pp. 38–39.

10. *Ibid.*, p. 46.

11. *Ibid.*, p. 46.

12. *Ibid.*, p. 59.

13. *Ibid.*, p. 14.
14. *Ibid.*, XVIII, p. 221.
15. *Journal*, p. 250.
16. *Ibid.*, p. 250.
17. G. Guisan (ed.), *op. cit.*, V, p. 267.
18. *Oeuvres complètes*, VIII, p. 51.
19. *Ibid.*, VI, p. 73.
20. *Ibid.*, p. 68.
21. *Ibid.*, XVIII, p. 54.
22. *Ibid.*, p. 57.
23. *Ibid.*, p. 74.
24. *Ibid.*, p. 75.
25. *Ibid.*, p. 84.
26. *Ibid.*, VII, p. 125.
27. *Les Grands Moments du XIXe siècle français*, p. 231.
28. *Ibid.*, p. 287.
29. *Oeuvres complètes*, X, p. 34.
30. The French text appears in *Oeuvres complètes*, X:
"On ne fait de la poésie qu'avec l'antipoétique.
On ne fait de la musique qu'avec l'antimusical.
Nos vrais amis sont les gens de métier, et non pas ceux qu'on nomme des artistes.
L' "art", on sait ce que c'est: c'est du greffé sur du déjà greffé.
Or, comme tous les greffeurs savent, on ne greffe que sur le sauvage.
On ne greffe que sur le sauvageon: c'est comme ça que nous greffons."
31. *Ibid.*, p. 43.
32. *Ibid.*, p. 48.
33. *Lettres 1919–1947*, p. 104.
34. *Le Passage du poète*, p. 11.
35. *Ibid.*, p. 40.
36. *Ibid.*, p. 41.
37. *Ibid.*, p. 36.
38. *Ibid.*, p. 48.
39. *Ibid.*, pp. 93–94.
40. *Ibid.*, p. 123.
41. *Ibid.*, p. 190.

Chapter Three

1. *Les Nouvelles littéraires*, May 17, 1924.
2. *Cahiers de la Quinzaine*, 17, no. 1, 1926.
3. H. Barbusse, *L'Humanité*, June 2, 1926.
4. L. Cazamian, "Le temps dans le roman anglais contemporain," *Etudes Anglaises*, 3, 1939, p. 342.
5. *Découverte du monde*, pp. 168–169.
6. C.-F. Ramuz, "Sous la lune," *Journal de Genève*, September 4, 1905.

7. *La Grande Peur dans la montagne*, pp. 49–50.

8. *Le Passage du poète*, p. 59.

9. *La Grande Peur dans la montagne*, p. 15.

10. *Farinet*, p. 7.

11. *Derborence*, pp. 72–73.

12. Y. Guers-Villate, *Charles-Ferdinand Ramuz*, Paris, Buchet/Chastel, 1966, p. 142.

13. *Farinet*, pp. 51, 103.

14. Y. Guers-Villate, *op.cit.*, p. 157.

15. *La Grande Peur dans la montagne*, p. 196.

16. *Derborence*, pp. 37–38.

17. *La Grande Peur dans la montagne*, p. 196.

18. There is, however, the short article by I. Santschi-Bardet, the details of which I include in the bibliography.

19. *Farinet*, p. 66. The italics are my own.

20. *Carnet de C.-F. Ramuz*, p. 109.

21. *Derborence*, p. 28.

22. *Ibid.*, p. 231.

23. L. Spitzer, "Le style de Ch.-F.Ramuz: le Raccourci Mystique," *Agonia*, Spring 1944, p. 16.

24. *Derborence*, pp. 109, 114.

25. *La Grande Peur dans la montagne*, p. 58.

26. *Ibid.*, pp. 28–29.

27. O. Ducrot and T. Todorov, *Dictionnaire encyclopédique des sciences du langage*, Paris, Seuil, 1972, p. 403.

28. *La Grande Peur dans la montagne*, pp. 247–248.

29. *Ibid.*, p. 253.

30. *Oeuvres complètes*, XVII, p. 306.

31. *Derborence*, p. 42.

32. *La Grande Peur dans la montagne*, p. 159.

33. *Derborence*, pp. 115–117.

34. A. Thibaudet, *Gustave Flaubert*, Paris, Gallimard, 1968.

35. *Derborence*, p. 52.

36. *Farinet*, p. 131.

37. *Ibid.*, p. 158.

38. *Vide* C.H. Parsons, *Vision plastique de C.-F.Ramuz*, Quebec, Laval University Press, 1964.

39. *Derborence*, p. 189.

40. *Ibid.*, pp. 66–67.

41. *Journal*, p. 39.

42. *Derborence*, p. 171.

43. O. Ducrot and T. Todorov, *op.cit.*, p. 286.

44. *Oeuvres complètes*, XVIII, pp. 264–265.

45. "L'Ecrivain dans son pays," *La Gazette de Lausanne*, October 25, 1936.

46. *La Grande Peur dans la montagne*, p. 233.

47. G. Guisan, *C.-F. Ramuz ou le génie de la patience*, Geneva, Droz, 1958, p. 92.

48. *Derborence*, pp. 224–225.

49. *Ibid.*, p. 226.

50. *Ibid.*, pp. 228–229.

51. *Farinet*, p. 8.

52. *Derborence*, p. 91.

53. *La Grande Peur dans la montagne*, pp. 196–197. The italics are mine.

54. *Ibid.*, p. 146.

55. *Ibid.*, p. 55.

56. *Ibid.*, pp. 181–190.

57. M. Cressot, *Le Style et ses techniques*, Paris, P.U.F., 1963, p. 77.

58. *Ibid.*, p. 76.

59. R. Barthes, *Le Degré zéro de la littérature*, Paris, Gonthier, 1968, p. 30.

60. O. Ducrot and T. Todorov, *op.cit.*, p. 400.

61. G. Gougenheim, P. Rivera, R. Michéa, A. Sauvageot, *L'Elaboration du Français Fondamental*, Paris, Didier, 1964.

62. D. Haggis, *C.-F. Ramuz ouvrier du langage*, Paris, Minard, 1968, p. 33.

63. *Oeuvres complètes*, VII, p. 187.

64. *Joie dans le ciel*, p. 87.

65. *Oeuvres complètes*, XVIII, p. 187.

66. O. Ducrot and T. Todorov, *op.cit.*, pp. 398–399.

67. *Derborence*, pp. 60–61.

68. *La Grande Peur dans la montagne*, p. 250.

69. O. Ducrot and T. Todorov, *op.cit.*, p. 323.

70. *La Grande Peur dans la montagne*, pp. 52–53.

71. *Ibid.*, p. 127.

72. E. Littré, *Dictionnaire de la langue française*, Paris, Gallimard, 1904 (see "asseoir").

73. *La Grande Peur dans la montagne*, p. 147.

74. E. Littré, *op.cit.* (see "courir").

75. P. Robert, *Dictionnaire alphabétique et analogique de la langue française*, Paris, Société du Nouveau Littré, 1965 (see "courir").

76. A. Praplan, "Ramuz et la Bible," *Europe*, July-August 1967, p. 41. The extent of these parallelisms may be consulted in detail in this article.

77. *Farinet*, p. 138.

78. *Ibid.*, p. 184.

79. *Derborence*, pp. 208–209.

80. *Besoin de grandeur*, pp. 51–52.

81. *Ibid.*, pp. 45–46.

82. *Oeuvres complètes*, VII, p. 18.

83. *Derborence,* p. 229.

84. *La Grande Peur dans la montagne,* p. 55.

85. *Le Passage du poète,* p. 85.

86. *La Grande Peur dans la montagne,* pp. 15–16.

87. *Derborence,* pp. 212–213.

88. M. Merleau-Ponty, "Le Cinéma et la nouvelle psychologie", *Sens et Non-sens,* Paris, Nagel, 1966, p. 93.

89. *La Grande Peur dans la montagne,* pp. 99–100.

90. *Derborence,* p. 123.

91. *Farinet,* p. 123.

92. *La Grande Peur dans la montagne,* p. 23.

93. Much of the fragmentary material in this chapter on Ramuz's mature style is expanded and extended in my earlier study which limits itself to the questions of narrative technique throughout Ramuz's novels. *Vide* D. Bevan, *The Art and Poetry of C.-F. Ramuz,* Cambridge, Oleander, 1976.

Chapter Four

1. *Lettres 1919–1947,* p. 198.

2. *Une main,* p. 104.

3. *Lettres 1919–1947,* p. 269.

4. *Oeuvres complètes,* XV, p. 15.

5. *Ibid.,* p. 18.

6. *Ibid.,* p. 89.

7. *Ibid.,* p. 82.

8. *Ibid.,* p. 95.

9. *Ibid.,* p. 190.

10. Donald Haggis's book, the details of which appear in the Select Bibliography, gives a clear idea of the type and extent of these changes in at least some of Ramuz's writings.

Selected Bibliography

PRIMARY SOURCES
(Novels marked with asterisk)

(The first date is that of the original publication. The edition which follows is the one I have used.)

1903: *Le Petit Village*, in *Oeuvres complètes*, Vol. I, Lausanne, Rencontre, 1967.

*1905: *Aline*, Lausanne, Marguerat, 1968.

1906: *La Grande Guerre du Sondrebond*, in *Oeuvres complètes*, Vol. I, Lausanne, Rencontre, 1967.

*1907: *Les Circonstances de la vie*, in *Oeuvres complètes*, Vol. II, Lausanne, Rencontre, 1967.

1908: *Le Village dans la montagne*, in *Oeuvres complètes*, Vol. III, Lausanne, Rencontre, 1967.

*1909: *Jean-Luc persécuté*, Paris, Grasset, 1966.

*1911: *Aimé Pache, peintre vaudois*, Lausanne, L'Age d'Homme, 1966.

*1913: *Vie de Samuel Belet*, Paris, Gallimard, 1944.

1914: *Raison d'être*, in *Oeuvres complètes*, Vol. VII, Lausanne, Rencontre, 1967.

1914: *Adieu à beaucoup de personnages*, in *Oeuvres complètes*, Vol. VII, Lausanne, Rencontre, 1967.

*1915: *La Guerre dans le Haut-pays*, in *Oeuvres complètes*, Vol. VI, Lausanne, Rencontre, 1967.

*1917: *Le Règne de l'Esprit malin*, in *Oeuvres complètes*, Vol. VIII, Lausanne, Rencontre, 1967.

*1917: *La Guérison des maladies*, in *Oeuvres complètes*, Vol. VIII, Lausanne, Rencontre, 1967.

1917: *Le Grand Printemps*, in *Oeuvres complètes*, Vol. VII, Lausanne, Rencontre, 1967.

*1919: *Les Signes parmi nous*, in *Oeuvres complètes*. Vol. IX. Lausanne. Rencontre, 1967.

1920: *Histoire du soldat*, in *Oeuvres complètes*, Vol. IX, Lausanne, Rencontre, 1967.

1920: *Chant de notre Rhône*, in *Oeuvres complètes*, Vol. X, Lausanne, Rencontre, 1967.

1921: *Salutation paysanne*, in *Oeuvres complètes*, Vol. X, Lausanne, Rencontre, 1967.

*1921: *Terre du ciel* which becomes *Joie dans le ciel* (1925), Paris, Grasset, 1949.

*1922: *Présence de la mort*, in *Oeuvres complètes*, Vol. IX, Lausanne, Rencontre, 1967.

*1923: *La Séparation des races*, in *Oeuvres complètes*, Vol. XI, Lausanne, Rencontre, 1967.

*1923: *Le Passage du poète*, Lausanne, Marguerat, 1964.

*1925: *L'Amour du monde*, in *Oeuvres complètes*, Vol. X, Lausanne, Rencontre, 1967.

*1926: *La Grande Peur dans la montagne*, Paris, Grasset, 1947.

*1927: *La Beauté sur la terre*, Paris, Grasset, 1961.

1928: *Remarques* (originally *Six Cahiers*), in *Oeuvres complètes*, Vol. XVIII, Lausanne, Rencontre, 1967.

1929: *Souvenirs sur Igor Strawinsky*, in *Oeuvres complètes*, Vol. XVIII, Lausanne, Rencontre, 1967.

*1932: *Farinet*, Paris, Grasset, 1961.

*1932: *Adam et Eve*, in *Oeuvres complètes*, Vol. XIII, Lausanne, Rencontre, 1967.

1933: *Une main*, Paris, Grasset, 1933.

1933: *Taille de l'homme*, in *Oeuvres complètes*, Vol. XV, Lausanne, Rencontre, 1967.

*1934: *Derborence*, Paris, Grasset, 1966.

1935: *Questions*, in *Oeuvres complètes*, Vol. XV, Lausanne, Rencontre, 1967.

*1936: *Le Garçon savoyard*, Paris, Grasset, 1957.

1937: *Besoin de grandeur*, Paris, Grasset, 1954.

*1937: *Si le soleil ne revenait pas*, Paris, Mazenod, 1968.

1938: *Paris, Notes d'un Vaudois*, in *Oeuvres complètes*, Vol. XVII, Lausanne, Rencontre, 1917.

1939: *Découverte du monde*, Lausanne, Plaisir de Lire, 1970.

*1942: *La Guerre aux papiers*, Paris, Grasset, 1947.

1943: *René Auberjonois*, in *Oeuvres complètes*, Vol. XVIII, Lausanne, Rencontre, 1967.

1943: *Anthologie de la poésie française* (2 vols.), Paris, Corréa, 1943.

1945: *Journal*, Paris, Grasset, 1949.

1947: *Carnet de C. -F.Ramuz*, Lausanne, Mermod, 1947.

1947: *Nouvelles*, Paris, Grasset, 1947.

1948: *Les Grands Moments du XIXe siècle français*, Lausanne, Mermod, 1948.

1956: *Lettres 1900–1918*, Paris, Grasset, 1956.

1959: *Lettres 1919–1947*, Paris, Grasset, 1959.
1967– C. F. *Ramuz, ses amis et son temps*, Vols. I - VI. Lausanne,
1970: Bibliothèque des Arts, 1967–1970.
1970: *La Mort du grand Favre et autres nouvelles*, Lausanne, Livre du
Mois, 1970.

SECONDARY SOURCES

BEGUIN, ALBERT. *Patience de Ramuz*, Neuchâtel, La Baconnière, 1950.
An incisive and affectionate assessment of the Swiss author.
BEVAN, DAVID *The Art and Poetry of C. -F.Ramuz*, Cambridge Oleander,
1976. The only book in English to date on Ramuz, and one which
deals exclusively, but in very great detail, with his narrative
technique.
BEVAN, DAVID. "C.-F.Ramuz: the path of the antipoet," *Nottingham
French Studies*, Vol.XIV, No.1, 1975, pp. 20–30. A brief analysis of
Ramuz's rejection of traditional literature and substitution of that
which might have been considered anti-poetic.
BRINGOLF, THÉOPHILE. *Bibliographie de l'oeuvre de C.-F.Ramuz*,
Lausanne, Mermod, 1942. An exhaustive and utterly invaluable refer-
ence work to the early Ramuz.
CINGRIA, HÉLENE. *Ramuz, notre parrain*, Bienne, Boillat, 1956. While
rejecting the charges of regionalism the author does tend to insist on
Ramuz as a *French-Swiss* writer.
CORNUZ, JEAN-LOUIS. "C.-F.Ramuz et la présence de l'histoire," *Europe*,
July 1967, pp. 63–70. An excellent short study of Ramuz's methods of
expanding the time-period with which he associates his vision.
GUERS-VILLATE, YVONNE. *C.-F.Ramuz*, Paris, Buchet-Chastel, 1966. A
general survey of great clarity, but with some possible errors of judg-
ment in detail.
GUISAN, GILBERT. *C.-F.Ramuz, ou le génie de la patience*, Geneva, Droz,
1958. The best study in French.
GUISAN, GILBERT. *C.-F.Ramuz*, Paris, Seghers, 1966. The "doyen" of
Ramuz scholars insists predominantly here on Ramuz as poet. He includes several well-chosen texts.
GUISAN, GILBERT. "Note sur la critique ramuzienne," *Revue
neuchâteloise*, No. 38, 1967. A most useful summary of Ramuz criticism up to that date.
HAGGIS, DONALD. *C.-F.Ramuz, ouvrier du langage*, Paris, Minard, 1968.
A stimulating and scholarly examination of different editions of certain
of Ramuz's works. The method is most revealing.
HASSELRÖT, BJORN. "Ramuz et le patois", *Etymologica* (Tübingen), 1958,
pp. 303–357. A careful and convincing examination of Ramuz's bor-
rowings and originality in this area.
NICOD, MARGUERITE. *Du réalisme à la réalité*, Geneva, Droz, 1966. A

study which is particulary interesting on the crucial new departure announced in 1914.

PARSONS, CLARENCE. *Vision plastique de C.-F.Ramuz*, Quebec, Laval University Press, 1964. The book makes some telling remarks about the pictorial quality of Ramuz's narratives, but may push conclusions too far towards exclusiveness.

PRAPLAN, ALBERT. "Ramuz et la Bible," *Europe*, July 1967, pp. 40–52. Some valid comment on Ramuz's use of a specific historical parallelism.

ROUSSEAUX, ANDRÉ. "Le droit de mal écrire", *Le Figaro*, August 21, 1929, p.5. An early exposition of the "problem" of Ramuz's resolutely distinctive language.

SANTSCHI-BARDET, ISABELLE. "Recherches sur l'image dans l'oeuvre de C.-F.Ramuz," *Etudes de Lettres*, April 1967, pp. 70–105. The only study of Ramuz's use of figurative language, and therefore of interest.

SPITZER, LEO. "Le Style de C.-F. Ramuz: Le raccourci mystique," *Agonia*, Spring 1944, pp. 12–26. Inevitably a model of skillful analysis, but perhaps the conclusion is somewhat invalidated by a wider reading of Ramuz.

VERDAN, JACQUES. *Notes bibliographiques sur l'oeuvre de C.-F.Ramuz 1942–1966*, Lausanne, Fondation de C.-F.Ramuz, 1967. This continues where Bringolf left off and is obviously just as valuable.

ZERMATTEN, MAURICE. *Ramuz à Lens*, Bienne, Panorama, 1967. A very informative little volume on this most vital of Ramuz's experiences.

Index

137